The Ultimate

GOLF JOURNAL

Keeping My Game on Course

BY LISA BACH

CHRONICLE BOOKS
SAN FRANCISCO

The Ultimate Golf Journal *is dedicated to my father, William Bach, who gave me the greatest gift—a passion for the game of golf.*

Text © 2007 Lisa Bach
Illustrations © 2007 Arthur Mount

ISBN: 0-8118-5891-X
ISBN-13: 978-0-8118-5891-5
Design by FUSZION Collaborative
Illustrations by Arthur Mount
Typeset in Mrs Eaves and Trade Gothic
Manufactured in China

Chronicle Books endeavors to use environmentally responsible paper in its gift and stationery products.

Distributed in Canada by
Raincoast Books
9050 Shaughnessy Street
Vancouver, B.C. V6P 6E5

10 9 8 7 6 5 4 3 2 1

CHRONICLE BOOKS
680 SECOND STREET
SAN FRANCISCO, CA 94107
WWW.CHRONICLEBOOKS.COM

THE ULTIMATE GOLF JOURNAL
BELONGS TO:

Name:

Address:

Home Phone:

Office Phone:

Cell Phone:

E-mail:

USGA #:

Handicap:

Local Golf Course:

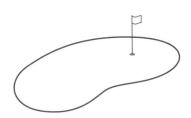

TABLE OF CONTENTS

INTRODUCTION

Even if you spend all day on the golf course hitting lousy shots, the moment you hit a single good one that "feels" right—then you're hooked. Golf is like that. Over the past twenty years, I've loved and hated the greatest game on earth. The times I've hated it were brief—mostly when I missed a gimmie or watched my shot sail right toward a small lake, or when I've wandered in the woods looking for my lost ball. But I still love the game, and I know that when I'm on the golf course I'm at my happiest and most inspired.

Golf can be all consuming. Can be?. All right, it *is* all consuming. When not on the course, we are often obsessed with the "stuff" of golf—the equipment, gear, magazines, tournaments, etc. You may find yourself playing "undercover golf" while driving around town (grip left hand on wheel to work on grip strength) or while cleaning up the yard (a rake can help you practice a proper backswing). Golf seeps into every aspect of your life and that's the beauty of it.

The Ultimate Golf Journal is the one place you can keep track of all aspects of your golf game *and* collect your most important golf memories. You no longer have to carry a golf bag stuffed with old scorecards, a tattered notebook with your random golf thoughts, or a wallet crammed with scribbled-down tee times and golf buddies' phone numbers. Now, you can keep track of practice information, scores, equipment, local courses, dream courses, your handicap, and more—all in one place.

And, if used as directed, *The Ultimate Golf Journal* will surely take strokes off your game, and isn't that the ultimate goal of every golfer? It's an astonishing feeling to break 100, and then 90, and then maybe one day, even 80.

Fore!

A BRIEF HISTORY OF GOLF

Throughout time, many nations have tried to claim golf as their own. The Scots. The Dutch. The Belgians. The French. Although many countries have similar games, no one can say for sure where or when the game we now know as golf was created. The Dutch contend that their traditional game, *kolven*, is proof that they originated golf, but the French have their own early predecessor, *jeu de mail*, and believe they founded it. But neither of those games involve a hole—which is why many believe Scotland should have the proud claim of founding golf, because the Scots have the distinction of their game utilizing a hole, and they can date it back at least as far as 1411, when the University of St. Andrews was founded.

The following is an abbreviated timeline of important events in golf history.

1457 James II of Scotland bans golf because it is interfering with military training—the Scots are at war with England and he needs his men to focus. The ban is lifted in 1502, when the Treaty of Glasgow is signed between England and Scotland.

1552 The first evidence of golf at St. Andrews links is recorded.

1567 The first known female golfer is seen—Mary, Queen of Scots.

1618 Wooden balls are used until this year, when the feathery ball is introduced. This new ball is a leather bag tightly stuffed with goose feathers.

1659 The first reference to golf in America, when Albany, New York, bans playing golf in the streets.

1759 St. Andrews becomes the first 18-hole golf course (and the standard for all courses) when during this year it is restructured and a few holes are combined so that the final total number of holes is 18.

1848 Robert Paterson of St. Andrews introduces the "guttie," a ball made of gutta sap. The balls were originally smooth, but eventually they are dimpled to improve distance.

1860 The British Open is held for the first time at the Prestwick Golf Club. Eight competitors play 36 holes in a single day and Willie Park Sr. wins with a score of 174.

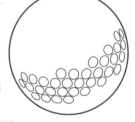

1894 The United States Golf Association (USGA) is founded.

1895 The USGA bans the pool cue as a putter.

1897 *Golf* is published for the first time and becomes America's first magazine focused on the sport.

First rubber-cored ball is patented and used by Coburn Haskell.

1902 William Taylor, from England, patents the first dimple-pattern golf balls.

1916 The first miniature (putt-putt) golf course opens in Pinehurst, North Carolina.

1930 At the age of 28, Bobby Jones Jr. wins his fifth U.S. Amateur golf title (his others were 1924, 1925, 1927, and 1928) and goes on to win the U.S. Open, British Open, and British Amateur, achieving what was then the Grand Slam of golf. He retires from competitive golf without ever turning pro.

1932 The sand wedge is introduced by Gene Sarazen, an American pro golfer.

1933 Hershey Chocolate Company sponsors the Hershey Open, becoming the first corporate sponsor of a professional golf tournament.

1934 The first Masters is played, and Horton Smith becomes the first champion.

1938 The USGA institutes the 14-club rule.

1942 The U.S. government stops all manufacturing of golf equipment for the duration of World War II.

1945 Byron Nelson wins 18 tournaments and sets an all-time PGA Tour record. During this year, he also plays an unbelievable 19 consecutive rounds shooting under 70.

1946 The U.S. Women's Open is instituted, and Patty Berg becomes the first champion.

1947 The U.S. Open is televised, making it the first golf event ever to be seen on TV.

1950 The Ladies Professional Golf Association (LPGA) is founded, replacing the ailing Women's Professional Golf Association.

1952 Patty Berg shoots an incredible LPGA record-setting score of 64 for an 18-hole round.

1953 Ben Hogan wins the first three legs of the modern Grand Slam (The Masters, U.S. Open, and British Open) but then does not compete in the final tournament for the Slam—the PGA Championship.

1954 After numerous complaints about the difficulty of the par 3 fourth hole at Baltusrol, where the U.S. Open is played, the architect, Robert Trent Jones, plays the hole. He shoots a hole-in-one.

1960   Major change in the Rules of Golf regarding putting—golfers are now allowed to pick up and clean their balls, and repair ball marks on the putting green.

1963   For the first time ever, a golfer earns more than $100,000 in prize money in one calendar year. Go, Arnold Palmer!

Mickey Wright wins a record 13 events in one year, winning 41 percent of all of the LPGA tournaments. She is the highest earner on the LPGA for the year, winning $31,269.

1967   Charlie Sifford wins the Greater Hartford Open and becomes the first African-American to win a PGA tournament.

1972   Alan Shepard sneaks a 6-iron on board the *Apollo 14* and hits a golf ball on the moon. It goes for "miles and miles and miles."

1974   Mike Austin really nails his drive—a 515-yard shot at the National Seniors Open in Las Vegas, Nevada. This is the longest drive ever recorded in a professional tournament.

1975   Lee Trevino, Jerry Heard, and Bobby Nichols have a brush with death during a storm when they are struck by lightning at the Western Open in Oak Brook, Illinois.

1976   Richard Stanwood takes the fewest putts ever in a round of golf—15!—at the Riverside Golf Course in Pocatello, Idaho.

1977   The acclaimed British Open takes place, where Tom Watson defeats Jack Nicklaus by one stroke. This is considered one of the most exciting tournaments in the history of golf.

A new PGA Tour 18-hole record is established by Al Geiberger when he shoots a 59 during the second round of the Danny Thomas Memphis Classic.

1979   Gary Adams, founder of TaylorMade, releases metal woods to the golfers of the world.

1980   The Senior PGA Tour is created.

The first woman crosses over the $1 million dollar mark in career prize earnings—the honor goes to Kathy Whitworth.

The fastest round of golf is completed when Gary Wright plays 18 holes at the Tewantin Noosa Golf Course in Australia in 28 minutes and 9 seconds.

1986   Jack Nicklaus wins the Masters for a record sixth time. His extraordinary win comes 23 years after he won for the first time in 1963. He also won in 1965, 1966, 1972, and 1975.

1988 On the 14th hole of the U.S. Women's Open, to protest slow play, Lori Garbacz has her caddie go to a pay phone and order a pizza to be delivered to the 17th hole. When Garbacz and her caddie arrive at 17, the pizza is there, and they have time to eat it—as there are still two groups in front of them waiting to tee off.

1989 The longest putt holed during a major tournament goes to Nick Faldo, who sinks a gorgeous 100-foot putt. This amazing feat helps Faldo go on and win the Masters.

1992 Five rounds of golf in five countries—in one day! In 16 hours and 35 minutes, Simon Clough and Boris Janic complete 18-hole rounds of golf in France, Luxembourg, Belgium, the Netherlands, and Germany. And astonishingly, they walk each course.

1997 Tiger Woods, in his 42nd week as a professional golfer, becomes the youngest golfer ever to be ranked No. 1 in the world at 21 years and 24 weeks old.

1998 Don Athey of Bridgeport, Ohio, stacks nine golf balls vertically without the use of adhesives.

2000 Tiger Woods wins the U.S. Open with the largest victory margin of any major tournament—he wins by 15 strokes.

Karrie Webb is the LPGA leading money winner with $1,002,000 in earnings. This makes her the first woman to ever win more than a million dollars in one golf season.

2003 Big year for women—Annika Sorenstam becomes the first woman ever to compete in a men's professional golf tournament. Also during this year, at 13 years old, Michelle Wie wins the U.S. Women's Amateur Public Links and becomes the youngest person ever to win a USGA event for adults.

> SUPERSTITION
>
> *If a red ladybug is found on the golf course, Michelle Wie places it on her putter for good luck.*

2004 Vijay Singh ends Tiger Woods's five-year and four-week reign as No. 1–ranked player in the world.

2005 Tiger Woods wins the Open Championship, becoming only the second golfer ever to win each major more than once. Jack Nicklaus shares that honor.

Henry Epstein of Australia obtains the record for spinning a golf ball on a putter for 2 minutes and 22 seconds.

2006 Phil Mickelson wins the Masters for the second time in three years.

2007 *The Ultimate Golf Journal* is published.

GOLF GLOSSARY

19TH HOLE
the bar at a golf course or country club.

ACE
a hole-in-one.

ADJUSTED GROSS SCORE
a golfer's score after his or her handicap stroke allowance is applied.

AIRMAIL
a shot that sails over the green or intended target.

ALBATROSS
a score of three under par (very rare). Also known as a double eagle.

AMATEUR
a golfer who is a nonprofessional and is not paid for playing.

APPROACH
a shot hitting the ball up to a green.

APRON
the short grass or fringe around the green that separates it from the fairway or rough.

AWAY
the ball farthest from the hole, and the one next to be played.

BACKSPIN
backward rotation of the ball in flight, which enables a ball to hit a green and then roll back.

BACK NINE
the last nine holes of an 18-hole golf course.

BANANA BALL
a bad golf shot—a slice—in which the path of the ball curves like a banana.

BEACH
a sand trap.

BIRDIE
a score of one under par.

BOGEY
a score of one over par.

BUNKER
a sand trap.

BUZZARD
a score of two over par. Also known as a double bogey.

CADDIE
a person who carries a golf bag for the player during a round of golf, and who may also give the player advice.

CARPET
the fairway.

CASUAL WATER
standing water on a golf course that is not an official water hazard, and from which the player can take unpenalized relief under the Rules of Golf.

CHILI-DIP
to catch a shot fat by hitting the ground before the ball. A bad golf shot.

CHIP-AND-RUN
a chip shot including the roll toward the hole.

CUP
the hole.

DEUCE
a score of two on a golf hole.

DIVOT
a portion of the grass that is ripped out of the ground by the head of the golf club during a swing (regardless of whether it is a practice swing or when the ball is contacted).

DOGLEG
an angle, turn, or bend in the fairway before the green is revealed.

DRAIN
to sink a putt.

DRAW
for right-handed players, hitting the ball and creating a sidespin so that there is a noticeable curve to the left. Curve to the right is called a fade.

DROP
dropping a golf ball on a hole when the player's ball is hit out of bounds or into a water hazard, or is unplayable.

DUFFER
an unskilled golfer. Also known as a hacker.

EAGLE
a score of two under par on a hole.

FAIRWAY
the cleanly mowed grass that makes up the main avenue from the tee box to the green.

FAT
when a golfer hits the ball below its center.

FLAG OR FLAGSTICK
a stick or "pin" with a marker showing the position of the hole on the green.

FORE!
a word yelled in order to warn other golfers to look out for a ball headed their way.

FRIED EGG
a ball that lands hard in a sand trap and is half buried in the sand.

FRONT
the first nine holes of an 18-hole golf course.

GALLERY
the audience watching a match or tournament.

GIMMIE
"give it to me" (don't make me putt it out). A short putt that is conceded so the player doesn't have to hole out.

GOLF WIDOW
a person who is neglected because of his or her significant other's love of golf.

GRAIN
the overall direction the blades of grass grow on a green.

GREEN FEE
the amount charged to play a round of golf.

HACK OR HACKER
an unskilled or uneducated golfer who shoots very high scores.

HAND WEDGE
the use of one's hand to improve one's lie. A foot wedge is also available.

HAZARD
a difficult feature on a golf course, considered to be part of the inherent challenge of the course. No relief is given for such features, including bunkers, permanent water, cart paths, etc.

HOLE-IN-ONE
a drive that is hit off the tee and goes directly in the hole. A hole that is played in only one stroke.

HONOR
the privilege of teeing off first. This is given to the winner of each previous hole.

HOOK
a shot that is hit by a right-handed player that curves strongly from right to left, starting in a path that is far right of the target and then coming back left and on target. The converse is true for a left-handed player.

IN THE LUMBERYARD
in the trees.

INSURANCE CLAIM
a very poorly hit shot (usually a slice or a wicked hook) that ends up causing some sort of damage to the golf course or a neighboring homeowner's property.

KNEE-KNOCKER
a short, challenging putt.

LAYUP
a shot that a player decides to leave short in order to play it safe—whether there is water or another hazard that could cause the player to hit above par.

LIE
the stationary position of a ball in play on the course.

LINE
the correct path of the ball to the hole on the putting green.

LINKS
originally, a golf course laid out on traditional Scottish rough seaside terrain; now people often mistakenly use the term to refer to any golf course.

LIP
the edge of the hole.

LOFT
refers to the angle of the clubface on a golf club, or a shot played so that the ball flies in a high arc.

MISREAD
to read incorrectly. This often refers to one's inability to read the line of a putt or the slope of a green.

MULLIGAN
when a player is allowed to replay any one shot on one hole. A "do-over."

OB
abbreviation for "out of bounds"; the area lying out of the area of play on a hole. A ball hit beyond the designated boundaries is OB.

PAR
the hole par is measured by the number of shots needed to reach the green plus two putts.

PEG
a tee.

PENALTY STROKE
a stroke added to a player's score due to a rule infringement, taking relief from a hazard or an unplayable lie.

PIN
another name for the flagstick.

PIN-HIGH
a ball that is level with the flagstick.

PITCH-AND-PUTT
a small golf course that is designed for chipping off the tee and then putting. Usually the course is made up of only par 3s.

PROVISIONAL
when a ball is thought to be out of bounds or lost, the player hits another ball to save time.

PULL
for a right-handed player, a ball that is hit and travels left of target. The converse is true for a left-handed player.

PULL CART
a two- or three-wheeled cart that holds a golf bag that can be pulled around the golf course.

READ

the process of evaluating or surveying the line of a putt to determine its break and speed.

RECOVERY

a shot that is played to rescue oneself from a difficult (lousy) previous shot, and to position oneself in a much better lie.

RELIEF

permission to lift and drop the golf ball, usually without penalty.

ROUGH

the area with heavier or thicker grass that surrounds the fairway.

RUB

an accident that moves or stops the ball with good or bad consequences. No relief is given.

SAND TRAP

a sand hazard on the golf course. Also known as a trap or bunker.

SANDBAGGER

a golfer who lies about his true playing abilities, making himself seem worse than he is in order to gain advantage in tournaments or bets.

SCRATCH

someone who consistently shoots par and has a zero handicap.

SETUP

a golfer's position when addressing the ball.

SHAG BAG

a bag used to pick up and store practice balls.

SHANK

a horrible shot when the ball is hit with the neck of the golf club rather than the face.

SINK

to hole a putt.

SKULL

a poor shot where the ball is contacted with the leading edge of an iron.

SLICE

for a right-handed player, a shot that curves dramatically from left to right. A slice differs from a fade in the degree to which the ball curves, and a slice is rarely played intentionally.

SNOWMAN

a score of eight on a golf hole.

SUDDEN DEATH

at the end of a tournament when there is a tie, this is a form of playoff in which additional holes are played and the first one to win a hole wins the tournament.

SWEET SPOT

the perfect place on a clubface to hit the ball.

TAP IN

to hole out a very short putt.

TEE

a small device that the ball is placed on for driving. Used only in the tee box area of each hole.

TEEING GROUND

the place from which the play of a hole begins.

THREE-PUTT

to take three putts to hole out on a green.

TOP

a shot where the ball is hit above its center.

UPHILL LIE

when the ball is at rest on a slope above the target.

WHIFF

a swing at the ball that misses entirely.

YIPS

continuous nervousness while putting or hitting the ball.

MY GAME

True or false: I am addicted to golf:

Person who introduced me to golf:

I was _____ years old the first time I played golf.

The first golf course I ever played:

My first golf clubs:

My current golf clubs:

My wood head covers (animals, socks, etc.):

My favorite golf ball:

Ball marker I use on the putting green:

My current handicap:

My longest drive:

My favorite day to play golf:

My preferred tee-off time:

Walk or ride:

How often I go to the range:

Shorts, pants, or knickers:

Collared shirt or T-shirt:

Hat or visor:

Black, blue, white, or red tee:

Glove or no glove:

> *I have a tip that can take five strokes off anyone's golf game: It's called an eraser.*
>
> —Arnold Palmer

Person I would most like to teach golf:

Last person I would want to play with:

Golf rule I break most often:

Golf rule I never break:

How often I take a "gimmie":

Number of golf balls I lose during an average round of golf:

How long I'll spend looking for a lost golf ball:

The longest putt I've ever sunk:

The shortest putt I've ever missed:

True or false: I use my hand wedge:

Number of utility (hybrid/iron-woods/wood-irons) clubs in my bag:

My grip is (circle one): overlapping / interlocking / ten-fingered

Worst weather I've ever played in:

True or false: My favorite hole is the 19th:

Number of times while at the range I've aimed
my shots at the poor guy in the ball-retrieving cart:

My lowest score ever for eighteen holes:

Highest score ever for one hole:

How many golf lessons I've taken:

The funniest thing that has ever happened on the golf course:

True or false: I've been to golf camp:

The last time I yelled "Fore!":

My best golf shot ever:

A golf club I couldn't play without:

The golf club I hit the worst:

What breaks my focus most on the golf course:

A golf course I dream of playing:

True or false: My vacations are planned around golf:

My favorite vacation golf course:

Most expensive round of golf I've ever played:

How often I watch golf on television:

The last professional golf tournament I attended:

The last golf tournament I participated in:

The best golf tip anyone ever gave me:

A golfer I greatly admire:

My ultimate foursome would include:

My favorite golf buddy:

The one golfer I'd like to beat:

A person I've let beat me:

What I always eat and drink on the course:

What I eat and drink while at the 19th Hole:

The golf brand I favor most:

Golf magazines I subscribe to:

My biggest golf superstition (lucky socks, foreign coin as marker, etc.):

GOLF FACT

The standardized golf hole is 4.25 inches in diameter.

Golf hazard I fear the most:

Most money won on a golf course:

True or false: I never improve my lie:

Number of golf clubs broken or thrown into trees/water:

Bet or no bet:

BYOB or buy on the course:

Most drinks consumed during 18 holes (that I can remember):

Most-used obscenity while on the golf course:

How competitive I am:

Cigar or no cigar:

Amount of rain to fall before I quit:

Best golf gadget I ever bought:

Golf gadget I never should have purchased:

Worst golf-themed present I've ever given:

The last golf gift I received:

MY TOP-FIVE LISTS

TOP-FIVE FAVORITE GOLF MOVIES

1. _____

2. _____

3. _____

4. _____

5. _____

Caddyshack | The Legend of Bagger Vance | Tin Cup
Babe | Follow the Sun | Happy Gilmore
Dead Solid Perfect | Gentleman's Game
The Caddy | The Greatest Game Ever Played

TOP-FIVE MOST-REFERRED-TO GOLF INSTRUCTION BOOKS

1. _____

2. _____

3. _____

4. _____

5. _____

Ben Hogan's Five Lessons by Ben Hogan (1957)
Golf My Way by Jack Nicklaus (1974) | *The Golf Swing*
by David Leadbetter (1990) | *How to Play Your Best*
Golf All the Time by Tommy Armour (1953)
Dave Pelz's Short Game Bible by David Pelz (1999)

TOP-FIVE ULTIMATE GOLF READS

1. _____

2. _____

3. _____

4. _____

5. _____

Bernard Darwin on Golf by Bernard Darwin,
edited by Jeff Silverman (2003)
Golf in the Kingdom by Michael Murphy (1972)
The Golf Omnibus by P.G. Wodehouse (1974)
The Story of American Golf by Herbert Warren
Wind (1948) | *Harvey Penick's Little Red Book*
by Harvey Penick with Bud Shrake (1992)

TOP-FIVE MOST-PLAYED GOLF COURSES

1. _____

2. _____

3. _____

4. _____

5. _____

TOP-FIVE DREAM GOLF COURSES

1.

2.

3.

4.

5.

St. Andrews (Old) *St. Andrews, Scotland*
Augusta National Golf Course *Augusta, Georgia*
Cypress Point Club *Pebble Beach, California*
Royal Melbourne Golf Course *Black Rock, Australia*
St. George's Golf & Country Club *Ontario, Canada*

GOLF FACT

Why do golf courses have 18 holes? Some say that during a discussion among the club's membership board at St. Andrews in 1858, one of the members pointed out that it takes exactly 18 shots to polish off a fifth of Scotch. By limiting themselves to only one shot of Scotch per hole, the Scots figured a round of golf was finished when the Scotch ran out.

TOP-FIVE GOLF MOMENTS

1.

2.

3.

4.

5.

TOP-FIVE GOLF WEB SITES

1.

2.

3.

4.

5.

www.usga.org | www.pgatour.com | www.lpga.com
www.thegolfchannel.com | www.golfweek.com
www.europeantour.com | www.golfforwomen.com
www.golfdigest.com | www.golf.com
www.golfonline.com

TOP-FIVE MOST-VISITED GOLF BLOGS

1. _____

2. _____

3. _____

4. _____

5. _____

www.thegolfblog.com | www.sirshanksalot.com
www.golfnomad.com | www.golfdash.com
www.hookedongolfblog.com

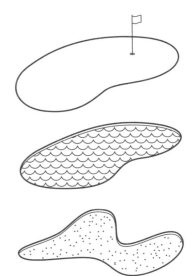

TOP-FIVE ALL-TIME FAVORITE PGA TOUR PLAYERS

1. _____

2. _____

3. _____

4. _____

5. _____

Jack Nicklaus | Tiger Woods | Arnold Palmer
Bobby Jones Jr. | Lee Trevino | Ben Hogan
Phil Mickelson | Vijay Singh | Tom Watson
Craig Stadler | Gary Player | Walter Hagen

TOP-FIVE ALL-TIME FAVORITE LPGA TOUR PLAYERS

1. _____

2. _____

3. _____

4. _____

5. _____

Nancy Lopez | Babe Didrikson Zaharias
Patty Berg | Kathy Whitworth
Annika Sorenstam | Michelle Wie | Beth Daniel
Mickey Wright | Amy Alcott
JoAnne Carner | Karrie Webb

MY GOLF BUDDIES

NAME:

Address:

Phone:

Cell:

E-mail:

Notes:

NAME:

Address:

Phone:

Cell:

E-mail:

Notes:

NAME:

Address:

Phone:

Cell:

E-mail:

Notes:

NAME:

Address:

Phone:

Cell:

E-mail:

Notes:

NAME:

Address:

Phone:

Cell:

E-mail:

Notes:

> *I know I can meet men a hundred times on a business or social footing and never know them, but once you go out on a golf course with a man and play the game with him, you know him. Golf to me has meant and always will mean a list of real friendships besides which all other successes of life are negligible. Of course, it's a great thing in my life, but the greatest thing in golf is friendship.*
> —Bobby Jones Jr.

NAME:

Address:

Phone:

Cell:

E-mail:

Notes:

NAME:

Address:

Phone:

Cell:

E-mail:

Notes:

NAME:

Address:

Phone:

Cell:

E-mail:

Notes:

NAME:

Address:

Phone:

Cell:

E-mail:

Notes:

NAME:

Address:

Phone:

Cell:

E-mail:

Notes:

NAME:

Address:

Phone:

Cell:

E-mail:

Notes:

NAME:

Address:

Phone:

Cell:

E-mail:

Notes:

NAME:

Address:

Phone:

Cell:

E-mail:

Notes:

NAME:

Address:

Phone:

Cell:

E-mail:

Notes:

NAME:

Address:

Phone:

Cell:

E-mail:

Notes:

NAME:

Address:

Phone:

Cell:

E-mail:

Notes:

NAME:

Address:

Phone:

Cell:

E-mail:

Notes:

GOLF COURSE:

Address:

Phone Number:

Web Site:

Fees:

Driving Range Hours:

GOLF COURSE:

Address:

Phone Number:

Web Site:

Fees:

Driving Range Hours:

GOLF COURSE:

Address:

Phone Number:

Web Site:

Fees:

Driving Range Hours:

GOLF COURSE:

Address:

Phone Number:

Web Site:

Fees:

Driving Range Hours:

> *I commit to a shot 100 percent and I don't worry about the result. What the ball does after it leaves the clubface is beyond my control, so I accept the outcome.*
>
> —Annika Sorenstam

GOLF COURSE:

Address:

Phone Number:

Web Site:

Fees:

Driving Range Hours:

GOLF COURSE:

Address:

Phone Number:

Web Site:

Fees:

Driving Range Hours:

GOLF COURSE:

Address:

Phone Number:

Web Site:

Fees:

LOCAL ACCOMMODATIONS:

Address:

Phone Number:

Web Site:

Room Rates:

LOCAL 19TH HOLES (NEARBY RESTAURANTS):

Restaurant Name:

Address:

Phone Number: Web Site:

Favorite Dish on Menu:

Best Cocktail or Beer:

Restaurant Name:

Address:

Phone Number: Web Site:

Favorite Dish on Menu:

Best Cocktail or Beer:

GOLF COURSE:

Address:

Phone Number:

Web Site:

Fees:

LOCAL ACCOMMODATIONS:

Address:

Phone Number:

Web Site:

Room Rates:

LOCAL 19TH HOLES (NEARBY RESTAURANTS):

Restaurant Name:

Address:

Phone Number:

Web Site:

Favorite Dish on Menu:

Best Cocktail or Beer:

Restaurant Name:

Address:

Phone Number:

Web Site:

Favorite Dish on Menu:

Best Cocktail or Beer:

GREAT GOLF MUSEUMS
AND COLLECTIONS
TO VISIT AROUND
THE WORLD

British Golf Museum
St. Andrews, Fife, Scotland

PGA Golf Hall of Fame
Pinehurst, North Carolina

Canadian Golf Museum
and Historical Institute
Aylmer, Quebec, Canada

American Golf Hall of Fame
Foxburg, Pennsylvania

James River Country Club Museum
Newport News, Virginia

Japan Golf Association Golf Museum
Tokyo, Japan

Jude E. Poynter Golf Museum
Palm Desert, California

GOLF COURSE:

Address:

Phone Number:

Web Site:

Fees:

LOCAL ACCOMMODATIONS:

Address:

Phone Number:

Web Site:

Room Rates:

LOCAL 19TH HOLES (NEARBY RESTAURANTS):

Restaurant Name:

Address:

Phone Number:

Web Site:

Favorite Dish on Menu:

Best Cocktail or Beer:

Restaurant Name:

Address:

Phone Number:

Web Site:

Favorite Dish on Menu:

Best Cocktail or Beer:

EQUIPMENT LOG

GOLF CLUBS

(Fourteen clubs is the USGA limit, so you may own more than you carry)

Driver

3-Wood

5-Wood

7-Wood

1-Iron

2-Iron

3-Iron

4-Iron

5-Iron

6-Iron

7-Iron

8-Iron

9-Iron

Pitching Wedge

Sand Wedge

Lob Wedge

Putter

Additional Clubs

> *What other people may find in poetry or art museums, I find in the flight of a good drive.*
> —Arnold Palmer

OTHER ESSENTIAL GOLF ACCESSORIES

FAVORITE GOLF BALLS Brand:

GOLF GLOVE Brand: Size:

GOLF SHOES Brand: Size:

BAG

PULL CART

ACCESSORIES LOG

I OWN THE FOLLOWING:

○ Club/Ball Washer ○ Distance Estimator

○ Golf Ball Retriever ○ Golf Shoes

○ Golf Shoe Bag ○ Head Covers for Irons

○ Head Covers for Woods ○ Push Cart/Golf Cart

○ Raingear/Rain Cover ○ Travel Bag

OTHER ITEMS:

○ _____ ○ _____

○ _____ ○ _____

○ _____ ○ _____

○ _____ ○ _____

GOLF EQUIPMENT WISH LIST

IF I PRACTICE REALLY HARD AND CROSS MY FINGERS, MAYBE I'LL GET THE FOLLOWING:

Driver:

Fairway Woods:

Irons:

Putter:

Glove:

Shoes:

Bag:

Pull Cart:

Golf Cart:

Other Golf Accessories:

> *Good judgment comes from experience, and a lot of that comes from bad judgment.*
>
> —Will Rogers

GOLF BAG ESSENTIALS

- ○ Ball Markers
- ○ Beer Opener
- ○ Cash for Food & Beverages (& Betting)
- ○ Golf Balls
- ○ Divot Tool
- ○ Sharpie (to mark ball)
- ○ Sunglasses
- ○ Tees
- ○ Umbrella

- ○ Band-Aids
- ○ Bug Spray
- ○ Club Cleaner
- ○ Hat/Visor
- ○ Pencils
- ○ Snacks (energy bar, peanuts, candy, etc.)
- ○ Sunscreen
- ○ Towel (attached to outside)
- ○ USGA Rules of Golf

OTHER ITEMS:

- ○ _____
- ○ _____
- ○ _____
- ○ _____
- ○ _____
- ○ _____
- ○ _____
- ○ _____

MY WARM-UP ROUTINE

Warming up before you hit the course is essential to shooting your best score. It's extremely important to stretch before you hit a basket of balls or play a round. Consider walking, neck rolls, shoulder stretches, side bends, twisting side-to-side, practice swings, visualization, meditation, and yoga.

To prepare both physically and mentally for my round of golf, I do the following:

> *Don't be in such a hurry.*
> *That little white ball isn't*
> *going to run away from you.*
> —Patty Berg

> *Golf combines two favorite American pastimes: taking long walks and hitting things with a stick.*
>
> —P.J. O'Rourke

MY DRIVING ROUTINE

Driving can often be the most nerve-racking swing in golf—not because of the difficulty of the swing, but because it occurs when all eyes are focused on you (think about teeing off on the first hole, where there are often many spectators). If you create a comfortable and reliable routine, you will gain confidence in your driving abilities and not fear duffing it in front of a crowd. This routine may also be your general routine for setting up to the ball to hit anywhere on the fairway or rough.

AN EXAMPLE OF A DRIVING ROUTINE:

- Stand back on the tee box and visual your drive.
- Find level turf and place the tee and ball in ground.
- Take a practice swing.
- Address the ball.
- Turn and reexamine the visualized drive.
- Adjust feet and body to line up with the target.
- Grip club and extend toward the ball.
- Focus on the ball.
- Swing.

MY STEP-BY-STEP DRIVING ROUTINE

1.

2.

3.

4.

5.

6.

7.

8.

9.

10.

MY PUTTING ROUTINE

Golf is a game of routines, and having your own putting routine is essential. Record your routine here, and refine it as you work on your game.

AN EXAMPLE OF A PUTTING ROUTINE:

- Mark, pick up, and clean ball.
- Place ball back down and remove marker.
- Step behind the ball and read the putt. If necessary, walk to other side of the hole and read the green.
- Visualize the line along which the ball will roll into the hole.
- Decide on the line and the speed.
- Approach the ball and set putting stance.
- Grip putter and take one practice swing before stepping up to the ball.
- Look at the ball and then visualize it rolling into the hole.
- Look back at the ball and putt.

MY STEP-BY-STEP PUTTING ROUTINE

1.

2.

3.

4.

5.

6.

7.

8.

9.

10.

Knowing each and every club in your bag is essential to playing the best golf you can, and the greatest place to learn about your clubs is on the golf range. Most golfers play more than they practice, but all golf professionals are clear about the fact that it's essential to practice more than you play.

Start out your visit to the range with your lowest-lofted club. Hit the wedge and take a series of 3/4 swings to loosen up, and then work your way through the clubs until you reach your longest club—your driver. Alternate each visit to the range by rotating even-number clubs with odd, so you can spend time with each club and get to know your distances. Remember to also spend time on the practice putting green.

> *The more I practice, the luckier I get.*
> —Gary Player

The charts that follow are to be filled out while at the golf range. Be sure to go to a range that has clear and accurate distance markers, so that you're confident the distances you're recording are correct. Remember to include every shot you hit with the club in your practice log—even if you top the ball and it only rolls 30 yards, note the 30-yard hit in your log. Also note the general direction of each shot—left, center, or right. Remember to mark this on your log sheet, as this will help you work on accuracy issues.

Your club distance will equal your median hit—not your average. To arrive at your median distance, list your ten distances in order from lowest distance to farthest. Add the fifth and sixth numbers together, and then divide by two. This figure is your median distance.

A few hints for the range:

- ◯ Wear a glove.
- ◯ Take time to think about the mechanics of your swing.
- ◯ Make adjustments to your swing and grip. The range is the ideal place for you to do so.
- ◯ Follow through and watch where the ball goes.

Once you've been to the range and filled in your practice logs, you'll see that when you are on the course, you will be much more confident with your club choices, and hopefully your score will improve!

DATE: _____   **LOCATION:** _____

CLUB	Swing 1	Swing 2	Swing 3	Swing 4	Swing 5	Swing 6	Swing 7	Swing 8	Swing 9	Swing 10	My Club Distance
OFF TEE											
SW	L C R	L C R	L C R	L C R	L C R	L C R	L C R	L C R	L C R	L C R	
PW	L C R	L C R	L C R	L C R	L C R	L C R	L C R	L C R	L C R	L C R	
9-IRON	L C R	L C R	L C R	L C R	L C R	L C R	L C R	L C R	L C R	L C R	
8-IRON	L C R	L C R	L C R	L C R	L C R	L C R	L C R	L C R	L C R	L C R	
7-IRON	L C R	L C R	L C R	L C R	L C R	L C R	L C R	L C R	L C R	L C R	
6-IRON	L C R	L C R	L C R	L C R	L C R	L C R	L C R	L C R	L C R	L C R	
5-IRON	L C R	L C R	L C R	L C R	L C R	L C R	L C R	L C R	L C R	L C R	
4-IRON	L C R	L C R	L C R	L C R	L C R	L C R	L C R	L C R	L C R	L C R	
3-IRON	L C R	L C R	L C R	L C R	L C R	L C R	L C R	L C R	L C R	L C R	
2-IRON	L C R	L C R	L C R	L C R	L C R	L C R	L C R	L C R	L C R	L C R	
7-WOOD	L C R	L C R	L C R	L C R	L C R	L C R	L C R	L C R	L C R	L C R	
5-WOOD	L C R	L C R	L C R	L C R	L C R	L C R	L C R	L C R	L C R	L C R	
3-WOOD	L C R	L C R	L C R	L C R	L C R	L C R	L C R	L C R	L C R	L C R	
ON TEE											
3-IRON	L C R	L C R	L C R	L C R	L C R	L C R	L C R	L C R	L C R	L C R	
5-WOOD	L C R	L C R	L C R	L C R	L C R	L C R	L C R	L C R	L C R	L C R	
3-WOOD	L C R	L C R	L C R	L C R	L C R	L C R	L C R	L C R	L C R	L C R	
DRIVER	L C R	L C R	L C R	L C R	L C R	L C R	L C R	L C R	L C R	L C R	
_____	L C R	L C R	L C R	L C R	L C R	L C R	L C R	L C R	L C R	L C R	

Notes:

DATE: _____ **LOCATION:** _____

CLUB	Swing 1	Swing 2	Swing 3	Swing 4	Swing 5	Swing 6	Swing 7	Swing 8	Swing 9	Swing 10	My Club Distance
OFF TEE											
SW	L C R	L C R	L C R	L C R	L C R	L C R	L C R	L C R	L C R	L C R	
PW	L C R	L C R	L C R	L C R	L C R	L C R	L C R	L C R	L C R	L C R	
9-IRON	L C R	L C R	L C R	L C R	L C R	L C R	L C R	L C R	L C R	L C R	
8-IRON	L C R	L C R	L C R	L C R	L C R	L C R	L C R	L C R	L C R	L C R	
7-IRON	L C R	L C R	L C R	L C R	L C R	L C R	L C R	L C R	L C R	L C R	
6-IRON	L C R	L C R	L C R	L C R	L C R	L C R	L C R	L C R	L C R	L C R	
5-IRON	L C R	L C R	L C R	L C R	L C R	L C R	L C R	L C R	L C R	L C R	
4-IRON	L C R	L C R	L C R	L C R	L C R	L C R	L C R	L C R	L C R	L C R	
3-IRON	L C R	L C R	L C R	L C R	L C R	L C R	L C R	L C R	L C R	L C R	
2-IRON	L C R	L C R	L C R	L C R	L C R	L C R	L C R	L C R	L C R	L C R	
7-WOOD	L C R	L C R	L C R	L C R	L C R	L C R	L C R	L C R	L C R	L C R	
5-WOOD	L C R	L C R	L C R	L C R	L C R	L C R	L C R	L C R	L C R	L C R	
3-WOOD	L C R	L C R	L C R	L C R	L C R	L C R	L C R	L C R	L C R	L C R	
ON TEE											
3-IRON	L C R	L C R	L C R	L C R	L C R	L C R	L C R	L C R	L C R	L C R	
5-WOOD	L C R	L C R	L C R	L C R	L C R	L C R	L C R	L C R	L C R	L C R	
3-WOOD	L C R	L C R	L C R	L C R	L C R	L C R	L C R	L C R	L C R	L C R	
DRIVER	L C R	L C R	L C R	L C R	L C R	L C R	L C R	L C R	L C R	L C R	
_____	L C R	L C R	L C R	L C R	L C R	L C R	L C R	L C R	L C R	L C R	

Notes:

DATE: _____ **LOCATION:** _____

CLUB	Swing 1	Swing 2	Swing 3	Swing 4	Swing 5	Swing 6	Swing 7	Swing 8	Swing 9	Swing 10	My Club Distance
OFF TEE											
SW	L C R	L C R	L C R	L C R	L C R	L C R	L C R	L C R	L C R	L C R	
PW	L C R	L C R	L C R	L C R	L C R	L C R	L C R	L C R	L C R	L C R	
9-IRON	L C R	L C R	L C R	L C R	L C R	L C R	L C R	L C R	L C R	L C R	
8-IRON	L C R	L C R	L C R	L C R	L C R	L C R	L C R	L C R	L C R	L C R	
7-IRON	L C R	L C R	L C R	L C R	L C R	L C R	L C R	L C R	L C R	L C R	
6-IRON	L C R	L C R	L C R	L C R	L C R	L C R	L C R	L C R	L C R	L C R	
5-IRON	L C R	L C R	L C R	L C R	L C R	L C R	L C R	L C R	L C R	L C R	
4-IRON	L C R	L C R	L C R	L C R	L C R	L C R	L C R	L C R	L C R	L C R	
3-IRON	L C R	L C R	L C R	L C R	L C R	L C R	L C R	L C R	L C R	L C R	
2-IRON	L C R	L C R	L C R	L C R	L C R	L C R	L C R	L C R	L C R	L C R	
7-WOOD	L C R	L C R	L C R	L C R	L C R	L C R	L C R	L C R	L C R	L C R	
5-WOOD	L C R	L C R	L C R	L C R	L C R	L C R	L C R	L C R	L C R	L C R	
3-WOOD	L C R	L C R	L C R	L C R	L C R	L C R	L C R	L C R	L C R	L C R	
ON TEE											
3-IRON	L C R	L C R	L C R	L C R	L C R	L C R	L C R	L C R	L C R	L C R	
5-WOOD	L C R	L C R	L C R	L C R	L C R	L C R	L C R	L C R	L C R	L C R	
3-WOOD	L C R	L C R	L C R	L C R	L C R	L C R	L C R	L C R	L C R	L C R	
DRIVER	L C R	L C R	L C R	L C R	L C R	L C R	L C R	L C R	L C R	L C R	
_____	L C R	L C R	L C R	L C R	L C R	L C R	L C R	L C R	L C R	L C R	

Notes:

DATE: _____ **LOCATION:** _____

CLUB	Swing 1	Swing 2	Swing 3	Swing 4	Swing 5	Swing 6	Swing 7	Swing 8	Swing 9	Swing 10	My Club Distance
OFF TEE											
SW	L C R	L C R	L C R	L C R	L C R	L C R	L C R	L C R	L C R	L C R	
PW	L C R	L C R	L C R	L C R	L C R	L C R	L C R	L C R	L C R	L C R	
9-IRON	L C R	L C R	L C R	L C R	L C R	L C R	L C R	L C R	L C R	L C R	
8-IRON	L C R	L C R	L C R	L C R	L C R	L C R	L C R	L C R	L C R	L C R	
7-IRON	L C R	L C R	L C R	L C R	L C R	L C R	L C R	L C R	L C R	L C R	
6-IRON	L C R	L C R	L C R	L C R	L C R	L C R	L C R	L C R	L C R	L C R	
5-IRON	L C R	L C R	L C R	L C R	L C R	L C R	L C R	L C R	L C R	L C R	
4-IRON	L C R	L C R	L C R	L C R	L C R	L C R	L C R	L C R	L C R	L C R	
3-IRON	L C R	L C R	L C R	L C R	L C R	L C R	L C R	L C R	L C R	L C R	
2-IRON	L C R	L C R	L C R	L C R	L C R	L C R	L C R	L C R	L C R	L C R	
7-WOOD	L C R	L C R	L C R	L C R	L C R	L C R	L C R	L C R	L C R	L C R	
5-WOOD	L C R	L C R	L C R	L C R	L C R	L C R	L C R	L C R	L C R	L C R	
3-WOOD	L C R	L C R	L C R	L C R	L C R	L C R	L C R	L C R	L C R	L C R	
ON TEE											
3-IRON	L C R	L C R	L C R	L C R	L C R	L C R	L C R	L C R	L C R	L C R	
5-WOOD	L C R	L C R	L C R	L C R	L C R	L C R	L C R	L C R	L C R	L C R	
3-WOOD	L C R	L C R	L C R	L C R	L C R	L C R	L C R	L C R	L C R	L C R	
DRIVER	L C R	L C R	L C R	L C R	L C R	L C R	L C R	L C R	L C R	L C R	
_____	L C R	L C R	L C R	L C R	L C R	L C R	L C R	L C R	L C R	L C R	

Notes:

DATE: _____   **LOCATION:** _____

CLUB	Swing 1	Swing 2	Swing 3	Swing 4	Swing 5	Swing 6	Swing 7	Swing 8	Swing 9	Swing 10	My Club Distance
OFF TEE											
SW	L C R	L C R	L C R	L C R	L C R	L C R	L C R	L C R	L C R	L C R	
PW	L C R	L C R	L C R	L C R	L C R	L C R	L C R	L C R	L C R	L C R	
9-IRON	L C R	L C R	L C R	L C R	L C R	L C R	L C R	L C R	L C R	L C R	
8-IRON	L C R	L C R	L C R	L C R	L C R	L C R	L C R	L C R	L C R	L C R	
7-IRON	L C R	L C R	L C R	L C R	L C R	L C R	L C R	L C R	L C R	L C R	
6-IRON	L C R	L C R	L C R	L C R	L C R	L C R	L C R	L C R	L C R	L C R	
5-IRON	L C R	L C R	L C R	L C R	L C R	L C R	L C R	L C R	L C R	L C R	
4-IRON	L C R	L C R	L C R	L C R	L C R	L C R	L C R	L C R	L C R	L C R	
3-IRON	L C R	L C R	L C R	L C R	L C R	L C R	L C R	L C R	L C R	L C R	
2-IRON	L C R	L C R	L C R	L C R	L C R	L C R	L C R	L C R	L C R	L C R	
7-WOOD	L C R	L C R	L C R	L C R	L C R	L C R	L C R	L C R	L C R	L C R	
5-WOOD	L C R	L C R	L C R	L C R	L C R	L C R	L C R	L C R	L C R	L C R	
3-WOOD	L C R	L C R	L C R	L C R	L C R	L C R	L C R	L C R	L C R	L C R	
ON TEE											
3-IRON	L C R	L C R	L C R	L C R	L C R	L C R	L C R	L C R	L C R	L C R	
5-WOOD	L C R	L C R	L C R	L C R	L C R	L C R	L C R	L C R	L C R	L C R	
3-WOOD	L C R	L C R	L C R	L C R	L C R	L C R	L C R	L C R	L C R	L C R	
DRIVER	L C R	L C R	L C R	L C R	L C R	L C R	L C R	L C R	L C R	L C R	
_____	L C R	L C R	L C R	L C R	L C R	L C R	L C R	L C R	L C R	L C R	

Notes:

DATE: _____ **LOCATION:** _____

CLUB	Swing 1	Swing 2	Swing 3	Swing 4	Swing 5	Swing 6	Swing 7	Swing 8	Swing 9	Swing 10	My Club Distance
OFF TEE											
SW	L C R	L C R	L C R	L C R	L C R	L C R	L C R	L C R	L C R	L C R	
PW	L C R	L C R	L C R	L C R	L C R	L C R	L C R	L C R	L C R	L C R	
9-IRON	L C R	L C R	L C R	L C R	L C R	L C R	L C R	L C R	L C R	L C R	
8-IRON	L C R	L C R	L C R	L C R	L C R	L C R	L C R	L C R	L C R	L C R	
7-IRON	L C R	L C R	L C R	L C R	L C R	L C R	L C R	L C R	L C R	L C R	
6-IRON	L C R	L C R	L C R	L C R	L C R	L C R	L C R	L C R	L C R	L C R	
5-IRON	L C R	L C R	L C R	L C R	L C R	L C R	L C R	L C R	L C R	L C R	
4-IRON	L C R	L C R	L C R	L C R	L C R	L C R	L C R	L C R	L C R	L C R	
3-IRON	L C R	L C R	L C R	L C R	L C R	L C R	L C R	L C R	L C R	L C R	
2-IRON	L C R	L C R	L C R	L C R	L C R	L C R	L C R	L C R	L C R	L C R	
7-WOOD	L C R	L C R	L C R	L C R	L C R	L C R	L C R	L C R	L C R	L C R	
5-WOOD	L C R	L C R	L C R	L C R	L C R	L C R	L C R	L C R	L C R	L C R	
3-WOOD	L C R	L C R	L C R	L C R	L C R	L C R	L C R	L C R	L C R	L C R	
ON TEE											
3-IRON	L C R	L C R	L C R	L C R	L C R	L C R	L C R	L C R	L C R	L C R	
5-WOOD	L C R	L C R	L C R	L C R	L C R	L C R	L C R	L C R	L C R	L C R	
3-WOOD	L C R	L C R	L C R	L C R	L C R	L C R	L C R	L C R	L C R	L C R	
DRIVER	L C R	L C R	L C R	L C R	L C R	L C R	L C R	L C R	L C R	L C R	
_____	L C R	L C R	L C R	L C R	L C R	L C R	L C R	L C R	L C R	L C R	

Notes:

DATE: _____ **LOCATION:** _____

CLUB	Swing 1	Swing 2	Swing 3	Swing 4	Swing 5	Swing 6	Swing 7	Swing 8	Swing 9	Swing 10	My Club Distance
OFF TEE											
SW	L C R	L C R	L C R	L C R	L C R	L C R	L C R	L C R	L C R	L C R	
PW	L C R	L C R	L C R	L C R	L C R	L C R	L C R	L C R	L C R	L C R	
9-IRON	L C R	L C R	L C R	L C R	L C R	L C R	L C R	L C R	L C R	L C R	
8-IRON	L C R	L C R	L C R	L C R	L C R	L C R	L C R	L C R	L C R	L C R	
7-IRON	L C R	L C R	L C R	L C R	L C R	L C R	L C R	L C R	L C R	L C R	
6-IRON	L C R	L C R	L C R	L C R	L C R	L C R	L C R	L C R	L C R	L C R	
5-IRON	L C R	L C R	L C R	L C R	L C R	L C R	L C R	L C R	L C R	L C R	
4-IRON	L C R	L C R	L C R	L C R	L C R	L C R	L C R	L C R	L C R	L C R	
3-IRON	L C R	L C R	L C R	L C R	L C R	L C R	L C R	L C R	L C R	L C R	
2-IRON	L C R	L C R	L C R	L C R	L C R	L C R	L C R	L C R	L C R	L C R	
7-WOOD	L C R	L C R	L C R	L C R	L C R	L C R	L C R	L C R	L C R	L C R	
5-WOOD	L C R	L C R	L C R	L C R	L C R	L C R	L C R	L C R	L C R	L C R	
3-WOOD	L C R	L C R	L C R	L C R	L C R	L C R	L C R	L C R	L C R	L C R	
ON TEE											
3-IRON	L C R	L C R	L C R	L C R	L C R	L C R	L C R	L C R	L C R	L C R	
5-WOOD	L C R	L C R	L C R	L C R	L C R	L C R	L C R	L C R	L C R	L C R	
3-WOOD	L C R	L C R	L C R	L C R	L C R	L C R	L C R	L C R	L C R	L C R	
DRIVER	L C R	L C R	L C R	L C R	L C R	L C R	L C R	L C R	L C R	L C R	
_____	L C R	L C R	L C R	L C R	L C R	L C R	L C R	L C R	L C R	L C R	

Notes:

DATE: _____ **LOCATION:** _____

CLUB	Swing 1	Swing 2	Swing 3	Swing 4	Swing 5	Swing 6	Swing 7	Swing 8	Swing 9	Swing 10	My Club Distance
OFF TEE											
SW	L C R	L C R	L C R	L C R	L C R	L C R	L C R	L C R	L C R	L C R	
PW	L C R	L C R	L C R	L C R	L C R	L C R	L C R	L C R	L C R	L C R	
9-IRON	L C R	L C R	L C R	L C R	L C R	L C R	L C R	L C R	L C R	L C R	
8-IRON	L C R	L C R	L C R	L C R	L C R	L C R	L C R	L C R	L C R	L C R	
7-IRON	L C R	L C R	L C R	L C R	L C R	L C R	L C R	L C R	L C R	L C R	
6-IRON	L C R	L C R	L C R	L C R	L C R	L C R	L C R	L C R	L C R	L C R	
5-IRON	L C R	L C R	L C R	L C R	L C R	L C R	L C R	L C R	L C R	L C R	
4-IRON	L C R	L C R	L C R	L C R	L C R	L C R	L C R	L C R	L C R	L C R	
3-IRON	L C R	L C R	L C R	L C R	L C R	L C R	L C R	L C R	L C R	L C R	
2-IRON	L C R	L C R	L C R	L C R	L C R	L C R	L C R	L C R	L C R	L C R	
7-WOOD	L C R	L C R	L C R	L C R	L C R	L C R	L C R	L C R	L C R	L C R	
5-WOOD	L C R	L C R	L C R	L C R	L C R	L C R	L C R	L C R	L C R	L C R	
3-WOOD	L C R	L C R	L C R	L C R	L C R	L C R	L C R	L C R	L C R	L C R	
ON TEE											
3-IRON	L C R	L C R	L C R	L C R	L C R	L C R	L C R	L C R	L C R	L C R	
5-WOOD	L C R	L C R	L C R	L C R	L C R	L C R	L C R	L C R	L C R	L C R	
3-WOOD	L C R	L C R	L C R	L C R	L C R	L C R	L C R	L C R	L C R	L C R	
DRIVER	L C R	L C R	L C R	L C R	L C R	L C R	L C R	L C R	L C R	L C R	
_____	L C R	L C R	L C R	L C R	L C R	L C R	L C R	L C R	L C R	L C R	

Notes:

DATE: _____ **LOCATION:** _____

CLUB	Swing 1	Swing 2	Swing 3	Swing 4	Swing 5	Swing 6	Swing 7	Swing 8	Swing 9	Swing 10	My Club Distance
OFF TEE											
SW	L C R	L C R	L C R	L C R	L C R	L C R	L C R	L C R	L C R	L C R	
PW	L C R	L C R	L C R	L C R	L C R	L C R	L C R	L C R	L C R	L C R	
9-IRON	L C R	L C R	L C R	L C R	L C R	L C R	L C R	L C R	L C R	L C R	
8-IRON	L C R	L C R	L C R	L C R	L C R	L C R	L C R	L C R	L C R	L C R	
7-IRON	L C R	L C R	L C R	L C R	L C R	L C R	L C R	L C R	L C R	L C R	
6-IRON	L C R	L C R	L C R	L C R	L C R	L C R	L C R	L C R	L C R	L C R	
5-IRON	L C R	L C R	L C R	L C R	L C R	L C R	L C R	L C R	L C R	L C R	
4-IRON	L C R	L C R	L C R	L C R	L C R	L C R	L C R	L C R	L C R	L C R	
3-IRON	L C R	L C R	L C R	L C R	L C R	L C R	L C R	L C R	L C R	L C R	
2-IRON	L C R	L C R	L C R	L C R	L C R	L C R	L C R	L C R	L C R	L C R	
7-WOOD	L C R	L C R	L C R	L C R	L C R	L C R	L C R	L C R	L C R	L C R	
5-WOOD	L C R	L C R	L C R	L C R	L C R	L C R	L C R	L C R	L C R	L C R	
3-WOOD	L C R	L C R	L C R	L C R	L C R	L C R	L C R	L C R	L C R	L C R	
ON TEE											
3-IRON	L C R	L C R	L C R	L C R	L C R	L C R	L C R	L C R	L C R	L C R	
5-WOOD	L C R	L C R	L C R	L C R	L C R	L C R	L C R	L C R	L C R	L C R	
3-WOOD	L C R	L C R	L C R	L C R	L C R	L C R	L C R	L C R	L C R	L C R	
DRIVER	L C R	L C R	L C R	L C R	L C R	L C R	L C R	L C R	L C R	L C R	
_____	L C R	L C R	L C R	L C R	L C R	L C R	L C R	L C R	L C R	L C R	

Notes:

DATE: _____ LOCATION: _____

CLUB	Swing 1	Swing 2	Swing 3	Swing 4	Swing 5	Swing 6	Swing 7	Swing 8	Swing 9	Swing 10	My Club Distance
OFF TEE											
SW	L C R	L C R	L C R	L C R	L C R	L C R	L C R	L C R	L C R	L C R	
PW	L C R	L C R	L C R	L C R	L C R	L C R	L C R	L C R	L C R	L C R	
9-IRON	L C R	L C R	L C R	L C R	L C R	L C R	L C R	L C R	L C R	L C R	
8-IRON	L C R	L C R	L C R	L C R	L C R	L C R	L C R	L C R	L C R	L C R	
7-IRON	L C R	L C R	L C R	L C R	L C R	L C R	L C R	L C R	L C R	L C R	
6-IRON	L C R	L C R	L C R	L C R	L C R	L C R	L C R	L C R	L C R	L C R	
5-IRON	L C R	L C R	L C R	L C R	L C R	L C R	L C R	L C R	L C R	L C R	
4-IRON	L C R	L C R	L C R	L C R	L C R	L C R	L C R	L C R	L C R	L C R	
3-IRON	L C R	L C R	L C R	L C R	L C R	L C R	L C R	L C R	L C R	L C R	
2-IRON	L C R	L C R	L C R	L C R	L C R	L C R	L C R	L C R	L C R	L C R	
7-WOOD	L C R	L C R	L C R	L C R	L C R	L C R	L C R	L C R	L C R	L C R	
5-WOOD	L C R	L C R	L C R	L C R	L C R	L C R	L C R	L C R	L C R	L C R	
3-WOOD	L C R	L C R	L C R	L C R	L C R	L C R	L C R	L C R	L C R	L C R	
ON TEE											
3-IRON	L C R	L C R	L C R	L C R	L C R	L C R	L C R	L C R	L C R	L C R	
5-WOOD	L C R	L C R	L C R	L C R	L C R	L C R	L C R	L C R	L C R	L C R	
3-WOOD	L C R	L C R	L C R	L C R	L C R	L C R	L C R	L C R	L C R	L C R	
DRIVER	L C R	L C R	L C R	L C R	L C R	L C R	L C R	L C R	L C R	L C R	
_____	L C R	L C R	L C R	L C R	L C R	L C R	L C R	L C R	L C R	L C R	

Notes:

DATE: _____ **LOCATION:** _____

CLUB	Swing 1	Swing 2	Swing 3	Swing 4	Swing 5	Swing 6	Swing 7	Swing 8	Swing 9	Swing 10	My Club Distance
OFF TEE											
SW	L C R	L C R	L C R	L C R	L C R	L C R	L C R	L C R	L C R	L C R	
PW	L C R	L C R	L C R	L C R	L C R	L C R	L C R	L C R	L C R	L C R	
9-IRON	L C R	L C R	L C R	L C R	L C R	L C R	L C R	L C R	L C R	L C R	
8-IRON	L C R	L C R	L C R	L C R	L C R	L C R	L C R	L C R	L C R	L C R	
7-IRON	L C R	L C R	L C R	L C R	L C R	L C R	L C R	L C R	L C R	L C R	
6-IRON	L C R	L C R	L C R	L C R	L C R	L C R	L C R	L C R	L C R	L C R	
5-IRON	L C R	L C R	L C R	L C R	L C R	L C R	L C R	L C R	L C R	L C R	
4-IRON	L C R	L C R	L C R	L C R	L C R	L C R	L C R	L C R	L C R	L C R	
3-IRON	L C R	L C R	L C R	L C R	L C R	L C R	L C R	L C R	L C R	L C R	
2-IRON	L C R	L C R	L C R	L C R	L C R	L C R	L C R	L C R	L C R	L C R	
7-WOOD	L C R	L C R	L C R	L C R	L C R	L C R	L C R	L C R	L C R	L C R	
5-WOOD	L C R	L C R	L C R	L C R	L C R	L C R	L C R	L C R	L C R	L C R	
3-WOOD	L C R	L C R	L C R	L C R	L C R	L C R	L C R	L C R	L C R	L C R	
ON TEE											
3-IRON	L C R	L C R	L C R	L C R	L C R	L C R	L C R	L C R	L C R	L C R	
5-WOOD	L C R	L C R	L C R	L C R	L C R	L C R	L C R	L C R	L C R	L C R	
3-WOOD	L C R	L C R	L C R	L C R	L C R	L C R	L C R	L C R	L C R	L C R	
DRIVER	L C R	L C R	L C R	L C R	L C R	L C R	L C R	L C R	L C R	L C R	
_____	L C R	L C R	L C R	L C R	L C R	L C R	L C R	L C R	L C R	L C R	

Notes:

DATE: _____ **LOCATION:** _____

CLUB	Swing 1	Swing 2	Swing 3	Swing 4	Swing 5	Swing 6	Swing 7	Swing 8	Swing 9	Swing 10	My Club Distance
OFF TEE											
SW	L C R	L C R	L C R	L C R	L C R	L C R	L C R	L C R	L C R	L C R	
PW	L C R	L C R	L C R	L C R	L C R	L C R	L C R	L C R	L C R	L C R	
9-IRON	L C R	L C R	L C R	L C R	L C R	L C R	L C R	L C R	L C R	L C R	
8-IRON	L C R	L C R	L C R	L C R	L C R	L C R	L C R	L C R	L C R	L C R	
7-IRON	L C R	L C R	L C R	L C R	L C R	L C R	L C R	L C R	L C R	L C R	
6-IRON	L C R	L C R	L C R	L C R	L C R	L C R	L C R	L C R	L C R	L C R	
5-IRON	L C R	L C R	L C R	L C R	L C R	L C R	L C R	L C R	L C R	L C R	
4-IRON	L C R	L C R	L C R	L C R	L C R	L C R	L C R	L C R	L C R	L C R	
3-IRON	L C R	L C R	L C R	L C R	L C R	L C R	L C R	L C R	L C R	L C R	
2-IRON	L C R	L C R	L C R	L C R	L C R	L C R	L C R	L C R	L C R	L C R	
7-WOOD	L C R	L C R	L C R	L C R	L C R	L C R	L C R	L C R	L C R	L C R	
5-WOOD	L C R	L C R	L C R	L C R	L C R	L C R	L C R	L C R	L C R	L C R	
3-WOOD	L C R	L C R	L C R	L C R	L C R	L C R	L C R	L C R	L C R	L C R	
ON TEE											
3-IRON	L C R	L C R	L C R	L C R	L C R	L C R	L C R	L C R	L C R	L C R	
5-WOOD	L C R	L C R	L C R	L C R	L C R	L C R	L C R	L C R	L C R	L C R	
3-WOOD	L C R	L C R	L C R	L C R	L C R	L C R	L C R	L C R	L C R	L C R	
DRIVER	L C R	L C R	L C R	L C R	L C R	L C R	L C R	L C R	L C R	L C R	
_____	L C R	L C R	L C R	L C R	L C R	L C R	L C R	L C R	L C R	L C R	

Notes:

DATE: _____ **LOCATION:** _____

CLUB	Swing 1	Swing 2	Swing 3	Swing 4	Swing 5	Swing 6	Swing 7	Swing 8	Swing 9	Swing 10	My Club Distance
OFF TEE											
SW	L C R	L C R	L C R	L C R	L C R	L C R	L C R	L C R	L C R	L C R	
PW	L C R	L C R	L C R	L C R	L C R	L C R	L C R	L C R	L C R	L C R	
9-IRON	L C R	L C R	L C R	L C R	L C R	L C R	L C R	L C R	L C R	L C R	
8-IRON	L C R	L C R	L C R	L C R	L C R	L C R	L C R	L C R	L C R	L C R	
7-IRON	L C R	L C R	L C R	L C R	L C R	L C R	L C R	L C R	L C R	L C R	
6-IRON	L C R	L C R	L C R	L C R	L C R	L C R	L C R	L C R	L C R	L C R	
5-IRON	L C R	L C R	L C R	L C R	L C R	L C R	L C R	L C R	L C R	L C R	
4-IRON	L C R	L C R	L C R	L C R	L C R	L C R	L C R	L C R	L C R	L C R	
3-IRON	L C R	L C R	L C R	L C R	L C R	L C R	L C R	L C R	L C R	L C R	
2-IRON	L C R	L C R	L C R	L C R	L C R	L C R	L C R	L C R	L C R	L C R	
7-WOOD	L C R	L C R	L C R	L C R	L C R	L C R	L C R	L C R	L C R	L C R	
5-WOOD	L C R	L C R	L C R	L C R	L C R	L C R	L C R	L C R	L C R	L C R	
3-WOOD	L C R	L C R	L C R	L C R	L C R	L C R	L C R	L C R	L C R	L C R	
ON TEE											
3-IRON	L C R	L C R	L C R	L C R	L C R	L C R	L C R	L C R	L C R	L C R	
5-WOOD	L C R	L C R	L C R	L C R	L C R	L C R	L C R	L C R	L C R	L C R	
3-WOOD	L C R	L C R	L C R	L C R	L C R	L C R	L C R	L C R	L C R	L C R	
DRIVER	L C R	L C R	L C R	L C R	L C R	L C R	L C R	L C R	L C R	L C R	
_____	L C R	L C R	L C R	L C R	L C R	L C R	L C R	L C R	L C R	L C R	

Notes:

DATE: _____ **LOCATION:** _____

CLUB	Swing 1	Swing 2	Swing 3	Swing 4	Swing 5	Swing 6	Swing 7	Swing 8	Swing 9	Swing 10	My Club Distance
OFF TEE											
SW	L C R	L C R	L C R	L C R	L C R	L C R	L C R	L C R	L C R	L C R	
PW	L C R	L C R	L C R	L C R	L C R	L C R	L C R	L C R	L C R	L C R	
9-IRON	L C R	L C R	L C R	L C R	L C R	L C R	L C R	L C R	L C R	L C R	
8-IRON	L C R	L C R	L C R	L C R	L C R	L C R	L C R	L C R	L C R	L C R	
7-IRON	L C R	L C R	L C R	L C R	L C R	L C R	L C R	L C R	L C R	L C R	
6-IRON	L C R	L C R	L C R	L C R	L C R	L C R	L C R	L C R	L C R	L C R	
5-IRON	L C R	L C R	L C R	L C R	L C R	L C R	L C R	L C R	L C R	L C R	
4-IRON	L C R	L C R	L C R	L C R	L C R	L C R	L C R	L C R	L C R	L C R	
3-IRON	L C R	L C R	L C R	L C R	L C R	L C R	L C R	L C R	L C R	L C R	
2-IRON	L C R	L C R	L C R	L C R	L C R	L C R	L C R	L C R	L C R	L C R	
7-WOOD	L C R	L C R	L C R	L C R	L C R	L C R	L C R	L C R	L C R	L C R	
5-WOOD	L C R	L C R	L C R	L C R	L C R	L C R	L C R	L C R	L C R	L C R	
3-WOOD	L C R	L C R	L C R	L C R	L C R	L C R	L C R	L C R	L C R	L C R	
ON TEE											
3-IRON	L C R	L C R	L C R	L C R	L C R	L C R	L C R	L C R	L C R	L C R	
5-WOOD	L C R	L C R	L C R	L C R	L C R	L C R	L C R	L C R	L C R	L C R	
3-WOOD	L C R	L C R	L C R	L C R	L C R	L C R	L C R	L C R	L C R	L C R	
DRIVER	L C R	L C R	L C R	L C R	L C R	L C R	L C R	L C R	L C R	L C R	
_____	L C R	L C R	L C R	L C R	L C R	L C R	L C R	L C R	L C R	L C R	

Notes:

DATE: _____ **LOCATION:** _____

CLUB	Swing 1	Swing 2	Swing 3	Swing 4	Swing 5	Swing 6	Swing 7	Swing 8	Swing 9	Swing 10	My Club Distance
OFF TEE											
SW	L C R	L C R	L C R	L C R	L C R	L C R	L C R	L C R	L C R	L C R	
PW	L C R	L C R	L C R	L C R	L C R	L C R	L C R	L C R	L C R	L C R	
9-IRON	L C R	L C R	L C R	L C R	L C R	L C R	L C R	L C R	L C R	L C R	
8-IRON	L C R	L C R	L C R	L C R	L C R	L C R	L C R	L C R	L C R	L C R	
7-IRON	L C R	L C R	L C R	L C R	L C R	L C R	L C R	L C R	L C R	L C R	
6-IRON	L C R	L C R	L C R	L C R	L C R	L C R	L C R	L C R	L C R	L C R	
5-IRON	L C R	L C R	L C R	L C R	L C R	L C R	L C R	L C R	L C R	L C R	
4-IRON	L C R	L C R	L C R	L C R	L C R	L C R	L C R	L C R	L C R	L C R	
3-IRON	L C R	L C R	L C R	L C R	L C R	L C R	L C R	L C R	L C R	L C R	
2-IRON	L C R	L C R	L C R	L C R	L C R	L C R	L C R	L C R	L C R	L C R	
7-WOOD	L C R	L C R	L C R	L C R	L C R	L C R	L C R	L C R	L C R	L C R	
5-WOOD	L C R	L C R	L C R	L C R	L C R	L C R	L C R	L C R	L C R	L C R	
3-WOOD	L C R	L C R	L C R	L C R	L C R	L C R	L C R	L C R	L C R	L C R	
ON TEE											
3-IRON	L C R	L C R	L C R	L C R	L C R	L C R	L C R	L C R	L C R	L C R	
5-WOOD	L C R	L C R	L C R	L C R	L C R	L C R	L C R	L C R	L C R	L C R	
3-WOOD	L C R	L C R	L C R	L C R	L C R	L C R	L C R	L C R	L C R	L C R	
DRIVER	L C R	L C R	L C R	L C R	L C R	L C R	L C R	L C R	L C R	L C R	
_____	L C R	L C R	L C R	L C R	L C R	L C R	L C R	L C R	L C R	L C R	

Notes:

DATE: _____ **LOCATION:** _____

CLUB	Swing 1	Swing 2	Swing 3	Swing 4	Swing 5	Swing 6	Swing 7	Swing 8	Swing 9	Swing 10	My Club Distance
OFF TEE											
SW	L C R	L C R	L C R	L C R	L C R	L C R	L C R	L C R	L C R	L C R	
PW	L C R	L C R	L C R	L C R	L C R	L C R	L C R	L C R	L C R	L C R	
9-IRON	L C R	L C R	L C R	L C R	L C R	L C R	L C R	L C R	L C R	L C R	
8-IRON	L C R	L C R	L C R	L C R	L C R	L C R	L C R	L C R	L C R	L C R	
7-IRON	L C R	L C R	L C R	L C R	L C R	L C R	L C R	L C R	L C R	L C R	
6-IRON	L C R	L C R	L C R	L C R	L C R	L C R	L C R	L C R	L C R	L C R	
5-IRON	L C R	L C R	L C R	L C R	L C R	L C R	L C R	L C R	L C R	L C R	
4-IRON	L C R	L C R	L C R	L C R	L C R	L C R	L C R	L C R	L C R	L C R	
3-IRON	L C R	L C R	L C R	L C R	L C R	L C R	L C R	L C R	L C R	L C R	
2-IRON	L C R	L C R	L C R	L C R	L C R	L C R	L C R	L C R	L C R	L C R	
7-WOOD	L C R	L C R	L C R	L C R	L C R	L C R	L C R	L C R	L C R	L C R	
5-WOOD	L C R	L C R	L C R	L C R	L C R	L C R	L C R	L C R	L C R	L C R	
3-WOOD	L C R	L C R	L C R	L C R	L C R	L C R	L C R	L C R	L C R	L C R	
ON TEE											
3-IRON	L C R	L C R	L C R	L C R	L C R	L C R	L C R	L C R	L C R	L C R	
5-WOOD	L C R	L C R	L C R	L C R	L C R	L C R	L C R	L C R	L C R	L C R	
3-WOOD	L C R	L C R	L C R	L C R	L C R	L C R	L C R	L C R	L C R	L C R	
DRIVER	L C R	L C R	L C R	L C R	L C R	L C R	L C R	L C R	L C R	L C R	
_____	L C R	L C R	L C R	L C R	L C R	L C R	L C R	L C R	L C R	L C R	

Notes:

DATE:

Location:

Pro:

Advice from Pro:

Important Lessons Learned:

Issues to Work On:

Suggested Drills/Exercises:

DATE:

Location:

Pro:

Advice from Pro:

Important Lessons Learned:

Issues to Work On:

Suggested Drills/Exercises:

DATE:

Location:

Pro:

Advice from Pro:

Important Lessons Learned:

Issues to Work On:

Suggested Drills/Exercises:

> *The reason the pro tells you to keep your head down is so you can't see him laughing.*
>
> —Phyllis Diller

DATE:

Location:

Pro:

Advice from Pro:

Important Lessons Learned:

Issues to Work On:

Suggested Drills/Exercises:

DATE:

Location:

Pro:

Advice from Pro:

Important Lessons Learned:

Issues to Work On:

> *If I could just putt.*
> *I might just scare*
> *somebody, maybe me.*
>
> —Jack Nicklaus

Suggested Drills/Exercises:

DATE:

Location:

Pro:

Advice from Pro:

Important Lessons Learned:

Issues to Work On:

Suggested Drills/Exercises:

DATE:

Location:

Pro:

Advice from Pro:

Important Lessons Learned:

Issues to Work On:

Suggested Drills/Exercises:

DATE:

Location:

Pro:

Advice from Pro:

Important Lessons Learned:

Issues to Work On:

Suggested Drills/Exercises:

DATE:

Location:

Pro:

Advice from Pro:

Important Lessons Learned:

Issues to Work On:

Suggested Drills/Exercises:

COLLECTED GOLF TIPS

Tips and wisdom gathered from lessons, books, magazines, and fellow golfers:

> *Of all the hazards,*
> *fear is the worst.*
>
> —Sam Snead

> *Golf is a game of misses,
> and the winners are those
> who have the best misses.*
>
> —Kathy Whitworth

> *If you're caught on a golf course during a storm and are afraid of lightning, hold up a 1-iron. Not even God can hit a 1-iron.*
>
> —Lee Trevino

What distinguishes golfers on the course, besides the ability to consistently sink a ten-foot putt? Good golf etiquette—because nothing is worse than playing with a golfer who doesn't respect it. The etiquette golfers show one another is key to enjoying a round of golf. The following are a few golden rules to remember while on the course:

Be on time. Arrive at least 15 minutes before your tee time. Better yet, arrive even earlier to warm up and hit a small bucket of balls at the driving range and putt on the practice green.

Always respect other players in your foursome. Keep discussions and noise to a minimum while on the tee box and green, and while other players are hitting. Also, be considerate of other golfers on the course by keeping your voice down, as greens and tee boxes are often close to one another.

GOLF FACT

Golf Financial News: 85% of golfers know the score of their last round of golf; 75% of golfers know their handicap; and only 52% know the current value of their portfolio.

Do not stand in the peripheral vision of the person teeing off. Watch each tee shot in order to be courteous and help other players find their ball.

If you lose your golf ball, look for it for a few minutes, but if there is a group behind you, be sure you don't hold up the course of play. Be courteous, and if you cannot find your ball—quickly process its loss, accept it, and drop another to continue play.

Keep a safe distance from other golfers while swinging your club, whether it's a practice swing or the real thing.

> *Drugs are very much a part of professional sports today, but when you think about it, golf is the only sport where the players aren't penalized for being on grass.*
>
> —Bob Hope

Do not hit your ball until you are sure that the group ahead of you is out of range. If you hit your ball and it is headed toward another player on the course, yell "Fore!" to warn them. Most golfers in earshot will duck and cover.

Always respect the proper order of play. On the first hole, the player with the lowest handicap usually tees off first. Once you've left the tee, the person whose ball is farthest from the hole hits next. On all subsequent holes, the player who won the previous hole gets the honor of teeing off first.

Replace all divots on the tee box or course, and repair ball marks on the green.

If you have extra time on the green while waiting for another player, it's always considered good luck to fix an extra ball mark on the green from a player who was not so considerate.

Keep the round moving by being prepared to hit your shot when it is your turn. You probably don't like waiting on other groups, so don't make other groups wait on you. Always try to keep pace with the group ahead of you, and if space opens in front of you, allow a faster group to play through.

Don't race golf carts or drive them unsafely. Rough driving and quick turns can cause serious injury or death.

THE PROFESSIONAL GOLF ASSOCIATION (PGA) MAJORS	THE LADIES PROFESSIONAL GOLF ASSOCIATION (LPGA) MAJORS
The Masters	
The United States Open Championship	*Kraft Nabisco Championship*
	McDonald's LPGA Championship
The British Open (The Open Championship)	*The United States Women's Open*
The PGA Championship	*The Women's British Open*

Observe cart rules. Some courses will post "cart path only" signs; others will ask you to observe the "90-degree rule." Respect the rules of the course.

Keep all golf carts—motorized or pull carts—off the greens and tee boxes. Also, keep your golf bag off the tee box.

Never yell or throw golf clubs in anger. Even if you want to scream out an obscenity or hurl your club into the lake (where it may meet up with your ball), please reconsider. This kind of behavior is unbecoming of a golfer, and can also be dangerous to others on the course.

If you enter a sand trap, do so at the point closest to your ball. After your shot, always rake your divot and footprints and make sure you leave the trap with no trace of your presence. Place the rake on the exterior of the sand trap, with the handle running parallel to the fairway.

If your ball is closest to the hole on the green, it is always considerate to tend or ask if the other players would like the flagstick removed. The Rules of Golf dictate that the ball may not strike the flagstick if hit from on the green, so tending or removing the flagstick is always a courteous gesture.

Mark your ball if it is in the line of another player on the green. When replacing your ball on the green, place it in front of the marker and then remove it.

Never... and I mean never... step in a player's line (on a green, the line between the ball and the hole). Always walk around or take a long step over another's player's ball path. Also, be conscious of your shadow on the putting green and ensure that it doesn't cast across another player's putting line.

By learning and respecting the proper etiquette of the game, you will surely avoid embarrassing golf mistakes on the course, and you will more likely be invited back to play with your friends. Unless, that is, you embarrassed yourself in ways unrelated to golf—in which case, you are on your own.

Columbus went around the world in 1492. That isn't a lot of strokes when you consider the course.

—Lee Trevino

GOLF EXPENSES

DATE	COURSE	9/18 HOLES?	GREEN FEE	CART FEE	19TH HOLE	OTHER (RANGE, ETC)
_____	_____	○ 9 ○ 18	$_____	$_____	$_____	$_____
_____	_____	○ 9 ○ 18	$_____	$_____	$_____	$_____
_____	_____	○ 9 ○ 18	$_____	$_____	$_____	$_____
_____	_____	○ 9 ○ 18	$_____	$_____	$_____	$_____
_____	_____	○ 9 ○ 18	$_____	$_____	$_____	$_____
_____	_____	○ 9 ○ 18	$_____	$_____	$_____	$_____
_____	_____	○ 9 ○ 18	$_____	$_____	$_____	$_____
_____	_____	○ 9 ○ 18	$_____	$_____	$_____	$_____
_____	_____	○ 9 ○ 18	$_____	$_____	$_____	$_____
_____	_____	○ 9 ○ 18	$_____	$_____	$_____	$_____
_____	_____	○ 9 ○ 18	$_____	$_____	$_____	$_____
_____	_____	○ 9 ○ 18	$_____	$_____	$_____	$_____
_____	_____	○ 9 ○ 18	$_____	$_____	$_____	$_____
_____	_____	○ 9 ○ 18	$_____	$_____	$_____	$_____
_____	_____	○ 9 ○ 18	$_____	$_____	$_____	$_____
_____	_____	○ 9 ○ 18	$_____	$_____	$_____	$_____
_____	_____	○ 9 ○ 18	$_____	$_____	$_____	$_____

DATE	COURSE	9/18 HOLES?	GREEN FEE	CART FEE	19TH HOLE	OTHER (RANGE, ETC)
_____	_____	○ 9 ○ 18	$_____	$_____	$_____	$_____
_____	_____	○ 9 ○ 18	$_____	$_____	$_____	$_____
_____	_____	○ 9 ○ 18	$_____	$_____	$_____	$_____
_____	_____	○ 9 ○ 18	$_____	$_____	$_____	$_____
_____	_____	○ 9 ○ 18	$_____	$_____	$_____	$_____
_____	_____	○ 9 ○ 18	$_____	$_____	$_____	$_____
_____	_____	○ 9 ○ 18	$_____	$_____	$_____	$_____
_____	_____	○ 9 ○ 18	$_____	$_____	$_____	$_____
_____	_____	○ 9 ○ 18	$_____	$_____	$_____	$_____
_____	_____	○ 9 ○ 18	$_____	$_____	$_____	$_____
_____	_____	○ 9 ○ 18	$_____	$_____	$_____	$_____
_____	_____	○ 9 ○ 18	$_____	$_____	$_____	$_____
_____	_____	○ 9 ○ 18	$_____	$_____	$_____	$_____
_____	_____	○ 9 ○ 18	$_____	$_____	$_____	$_____
_____	_____	○ 9 ○ 18	$_____	$_____	$_____	$_____
_____	_____	○ 9 ○ 18	$_____	$_____	$_____	$_____
_____	_____	○ 9 ○ 18	$_____	$_____	$_____	$_____
_____	_____	○ 9 ○ 18	$_____	$_____	$_____	$_____
_____	_____	○ 9 ○ 18	$_____	$_____	$_____	$_____

DATE	COURSE	9/18 HOLES?	GREEN FEE	CART FEE	19TH HOLE	OTHER (RANGE, ETC)
_____	_____	○ 9 ○ 18	$_____	$_____	$_____	$_____
_____	_____	○ 9 ○ 18	$_____	$_____	$_____	$_____
_____	_____	○ 9 ○ 18	$_____	$_____	$_____	$_____
_____	_____	○ 9 ○ 18	$_____	$_____	$_____	$_____
_____	_____	○ 9 ○ 18	$_____	$_____	$_____	$_____
_____	_____	○ 9 ○ 18	$_____	$_____	$_____	$_____
_____	_____	○ 9 ○ 18	$_____	$_____	$_____	$_____
_____	_____	○ 9 ○ 18	$_____	$_____	$_____	$_____
_____	_____	○ 9 ○ 18	$_____	$_____	$_____	$_____
_____	_____	○ 9 ○ 18	$_____	$_____	$_____	$_____
_____	_____	○ 9 ○ 18	$_____	$_____	$_____	$_____
_____	_____	○ 9 ○ 18	$_____	$_____	$_____	$_____
_____	_____	○ 9 ○ 18	$_____	$_____	$_____	$_____
_____	_____	○ 9 ○ 18	$_____	$_____	$_____	$_____
_____	_____	○ 9 ○ 18	$_____	$_____	$_____	$_____
_____	_____	○ 9 ○ 18	$_____	$_____	$_____	$_____
_____	_____	○ 9 ○ 18	$_____	$_____	$_____	$_____
_____	_____	○ 9 ○ 18	$_____	$_____	$_____	$_____
_____	_____	○ 9 ○ 18	$_____	$_____	$_____	$_____

OTHER GOLF EXPENSES

DATE	ITEM	AMOUNT
_____	_____	$_____
_____	_____	$_____
_____	_____	$_____
_____	_____	$_____
_____	_____	$_____
_____	_____	$_____
_____	_____	$_____
_____	_____	$_____
_____	_____	$_____
_____	_____	$_____
_____	_____	$_____
_____	_____	$_____
_____	_____	$_____
_____	_____	$_____
_____	_____	$_____
_____	_____	$_____
_____	_____	$_____
_____	_____	$_____
_____	_____	$_____

OTHER GOLF EXPENSES

DATE	ITEM	AMOUNT
_____	_____	$_____
_____	_____	$_____
_____	_____	$_____
_____	_____	$_____
_____	_____	$_____
_____	_____	$_____
_____	_____	$_____
_____	_____	$_____
_____	_____	$_____
_____	_____	$_____
_____	_____	$_____
_____	_____	$_____
_____	_____	$_____
_____	_____	$_____
_____	_____	$_____
_____	_____	$_____
_____	_____	$_____
_____	_____	$_____
_____	_____	$_____

GOLF LOG

Keeping track of your golf game can be an entertaining (and sometimes frustrating—did I really 5-putt?) experience. It's important to be mindful of your game—the number of strokes taken during a round, the number of fairways and greens hit in regulation, and your total number of putts. It is only when you sit down and copy your scorecard into the following register that you will begin to understand and strategize on the various aspects of your game. Maybe you 2-putted all day, but you just realized you didn't hit a single green in regulation. Look for trends in your game that you can work on—because only then will you be able to lower your golf score.

DATE: Tee Time:

Green Fees: $ Walk or Ride?

Weather:

Course Par: Course Yardage:

USGA Course Rating: USGA Course Slope:

Members of Foursome:

Notes:

Hole	Par	Yards	Handicap	Fairways Hit in Regulation	Greens Hit in Regulation	# of Putts	My Score	Player #2 _____ Score	Player #3 _____ Score	Player #4 _____ Score
1										
2										
3										
4										
5										
6										
7										
8										
9										
OUT										
10										
11										
12										
13										
14										
15										
16										
17										
18										
IN										
OUT										
TOTAL										

1 Putt	2 Putts	3 Putts	Other	Total Putts	My Average # of Putts this Round

Eagles	Birdies	Pars	Bogeys	Double Bogeys	Snowmen (8s) or Other

DATE: Tee Time:

Green Fees: $ Walk or Ride?

Weather:

Course Par: Course Yardage:

USGA Course Rating: USGA Course Slope:

Members of Foursome:

Notes:

Hole	Par	Yards	Handicap	Fairways Hit in Regulation	Greens Hit in Regulation	# of Putts	My Score	Player #2 _____ Score	Player #3 _____ Score	Player #4 _____ Score
1										
2										
3										
4										
5										
6										
7										
8										
9										
OUT										
10										
11										
12										
13										
14										
15										
16										
17										
18										
IN										
OUT										
TOTAL										

1 Putt	2 Putts	3 Putts	Other	Total Putts	My Average # of Putts this Round

Eagles	Birdies	Pars	Bogeys	Double Bogeys	Snowmen (8s) or Other

GOLF LOG

DATE: _____ Tee Time: _____

Green Fees: $ _____ Walk or Ride? _____

Weather: _____

Course Par: _____ Course Yardage: _____

USGA Course Rating: _____ USGA Course Slope: _____

Members of Foursome: _____

Notes: _____

_____

Hole	Par	Yards	Handicap	Fairways Hit in Regulation	Greens Hit in Regulation	# of Putts	My Score	Player #2 Score	Player #3 Score	Player #4 Score
1										
2										
3										
4										
5										
6										
7										
8										
9										
OUT										
10										
11										
12										
13										
14										
15										
16										
17										
18										
IN										
OUT										
TOTAL										

1 Putt	2 Putts	3 Putts	Other	Total Putts	My Average # of Putts this Round

Eagles	Birdies	Pars	Bogeys	Double Bogeys	Snowmen (8s) or Other

DATE: Tee Time:

Green Fees: $ Walk or Ride?

Weather:

Course Par: Course Yardage:

USGA Course Rating: USGA Course Slope:

Members of Foursome:

Notes:

Hole	Par	Yards	Handicap	Fairways Hit in Regulation	Greens Hit in Regulation	# of Putts	My Score	Player #2 Score	Player #3 Score	Player #4 Score
1										
2										
3										
4										
5										
6										
7										
8										
9										
OUT										
10										
11										
12										
13										
14										
15										
16										
17										
18										
IN										
OUT										
TOTAL										

1 Putt	2 Putts	3 Putts	Other	Total Putts	My Average # of Putts this Round

Eagles	Birdies	Pars	Bogeys	Double Bogeys	Snowmen (8s) or Other

DATE: Tee Time:

Green Fees: $ Walk or Ride?

Weather:

Course Par: Course Yardage:

USGA Course Rating: USGA Course Slope:

Members of Foursome:

Notes:

Hole	Par	Yards	Handicap	Fairways Hit in Regulation	Greens Hit in Regulation	# of Putts	My Score	Player #2 ___ Score	Player #3 ___ Score	Player #4 ___ Score
1										
2										
3										
4										
5										
6										
7										
8										
9										
OUT										
10										
11										
12										
13										
14										
15										
16										
17										
18										
IN										
OUT										
TOTAL										

1 Putt	2 Putts	3 Putts	Other	Total Putts	My Average # of Putts this Round

Eagles	Birdies	Pars	Bogeys	Double Bogeys	Snowmen (8s) or Other

DATE: _____ Tee Time: _____

Green Fees: $ _____ Walk or Ride? _____

Weather: _____

Course Par: _____ Course Yardage: _____

USGA Course Rating: _____ USGA Course Slope: _____

Members of Foursome: _____

Notes: _____

Hole	Par	Yards	Handicap	Fairways Hit in Regulation	Greens Hit in Regulation	# of Putts	My Score	Player #2 Score	Player #3 Score	Player #4 Score
1										
2										
3										
4										
5										
6										
7										
8										
9										
OUT										
10										
11										
12										
13										
14										
15										
16										
17										
18										
IN										
OUT										
TOTAL										

1 Putt	2 Putts	3 Putts	Other	Total Putts	My Average # of Putts this Round

Eagles	Birdies	Pars	Bogeys	Double Bogeys	Snowmen (8s) or Other

GOLF LOG

DATE: Tee Time:

Green Fees: $ Walk or Ride?

Weather:

Course Par: Course Yardage:

USGA Course Rating: USGA Course Slope:

Members of Foursome:

Notes:

Hole	Par	Yards	Handicap	Fairways Hit in Regulation	Greens Hit in Regulation	# of Putts	My Score	Player #2 _____ Score	Player #3 _____ Score	Player #4 _____ Score
1										
2										
3										
4										
5										
6										
7										
8										
9										
OUT										
10										
11										
12										
13										
14										
15										
16										
17										
18										
IN										
OUT										
TOTAL										

1 Putt	2 Putts	3 Putts	Other	Total Putts	My Average # of Putts this Round

Eagles	Birdies	Pars	Bogeys	Double Bogeys	Snowmen (8s) or Other

DATE: Tee Time:

Green Fees: $ Walk or Ride?

Weather:

Course Par: Course Yardage:

USGA Course Rating: USGA Course Slope:

Members of Foursome:

Notes:

Hole	Par	Yards	Handicap	Fairways Hit in Regulation	Greens Hit in Regulation	# of Putts	My Score	Player #2 _____ Score	Player #3 _____ Score	Player #4 _____ Score
1										
2										
3										
4										
5										
6										
7										
8										
9										
OUT										
10										
11										
12										
13										
14										
15										
16										
17										
18										
IN										
OUT										
TOTAL										

1 Putt	2 Putts	3 Putts	Other	Total Putts	My Average # of Putts this Round

Eagles	Birdies	Pars	Bogeys	Double Bogeys	Snowmen (8s) or Other

DATE: Tee Time:

Green Fees: $ Walk or Ride?

Weather:

Course Par: Course Yardage:

USGA Course Rating: USGA Course Slope:

Members of Foursome:

Notes:

Hole	Par	Yards	Handicap	Fairways Hit in Regulation	Greens Hit in Regulation	# of Putts	My Score	Player #2 Score	Player #3 Score	Player #4 Score
1										
2										
3										
4										
5										
6										
7										
8										
9										
OUT										
10										
11										
12										
13										
14										
15										
16										
17										
18										
IN										
OUT										
TOTAL										

1 Putt	2 Putts	3 Putts	Other	Total Putts	My Average # of Putts this Round

Eagles	Birdies	Pars	Bogeys	Double Bogeys	Snowmen (8s) or Other

DATE: Tee Time:

Green Fees: $ Walk or Ride?

Weather:

Course Par: Course Yardage:

USGA Course Rating: USGA Course Slope:

Members of Foursome:

Notes:

Hole	Par	Yards	Handicap	Fairways Hit in Regulation	Greens Hit in Regulation	# of Putts	My Score	Player #2 Score	Player #3 Score	Player #4 Score
1										
2										
3										
4										
5										
6										
7										
8										
9										
OUT										
10										
11										
12										
13										
14										
15										
16										
17										
18										
IN										
OUT										
TOTAL										

1 Putt	2 Putts	3 Putts	Other	Total Putts	My Average # of Putts this Round

Eagles	Birdies	Pars	Bogeys	Double Bogeys	Snowmen (8s) or Other

DATE: | Tee Time:

Green Fees: $ | Walk or Ride?

Weather:

Course Par: | Course Yardage:

USGA Course Rating: | USGA Course Slope:

Members of Foursome:

Notes:

Hole	Par	Yards	Handicap	Fairways Hit in Regulation	Greens Hit in Regulation	# of Putts	My Score	Player #2 _____ Score	Player #3 _____ Score	Player #4 _____ Score
1										
2										
3										
4										
5										
6										
7										
8										
9										
OUT										
10										
11										
12										
13										
14										
15										
16										
17										
18										
IN										
OUT										
TOTAL										

1 Putt	2 Putts	3 Putts	Other	Total Putts	My Average # of Putts this Round

Eagles	Birdies	Pars	Bogeys	Double Bogeys	Snowmen (8s) or Other

DATE: — Tee Time:

Green Fees: $ — Walk or Ride?

Weather:

Course Par: — Course Yardage:

USGA Course Rating: — USGA Course Slope:

Members of Foursome:

Notes:

Hole	Par	Yards	Handicap	Fairways Hit in Regulation	Greens Hit in Regulation	# of Putts	My Score	Player #2 Score	Player #3 Score	Player #4 Score
1										
2										
3										
4										
5										
6										
7										
8										
9										
OUT										
10										
11										
12										
13										
14										
15										
16										
17										
18										
IN										
OUT										
TOTAL										

1 Putt	2 Putts	3 Putts	Other	Total Putts	My Average # of Putts this Round

Eagles	Birdies	Pars	Bogeys	Double Bogeys	Snowmen (8s) or Other

DATE:

Tee Time:

Green Fees: $

Walk or Ride?

Weather:

Course Par:

Course Yardage:

USGA Course Rating:

USGA Course Slope:

Members of Foursome:

Notes:

Hole	Par	Yards	Handicap	Fairways Hit in Regulation	Greens Hit in Regulation	# of Putts	My Score	Player #2 _____ Score	Player #3 _____ Score	Player #4 _____ Score
1										
2										
3										
4										
5										
6										
7										
8										
9										
OUT										
10										
11										
12										
13										
14										
15										
16										
17										
18										
IN										
OUT										
TOTAL										

1 Putt	2 Putts	3 Putts	Other	Total Putts	My Average # of Putts this Round

Eagles	Birdies	Pars	Bogeys	Double Bogeys	Snowmen (8s) or Other

DATE: | Tee Time:

Green Fees: $ | Walk or Ride?

Weather:

Course Par: | Course Yardage:

USGA Course Rating: | USGA Course Slope:

Members of Foursome:

Notes:

Hole	Par	Yards	Handicap	Fairways Hit in Regulation	Greens Hit in Regulation	# of Putts	My Score	Player #2 Score	Player #3 Score	Player #4 Score
1										
2										
3										
4										
5										
6										
7										
8										
9										
OUT										
10										
11										
12										
13										
14										
15										
16										
17										
18										
IN										
OUT										
TOTAL										

1 Putt	2 Putts	3 Putts	Other	Total Putts	My Average # of Putts this Round

Eagles	Birdies	Pars	Bogeys	Double Bogeys	Snowmen (8s) or Other

DATE:

Tee Time:

Green Fees: $

Walk or Ride?

Weather:

Course Par:

Course Yardage:

USGA Course Rating:

USGA Course Slope:

Members of Foursome:

Notes:

Hole	Par	Yards	Handicap	Fairways Hit in Regulation	Greens Hit in Regulation	# of Putts	My Score	Player #2 Score	Player #3 Score	Player #4 Score
1										
2										
3										
4										
5										
6										
7										
8										
9										
OUT										
10										
11										
12										
13										
14										
15										
16										
17										
18										
IN										
OUT										
TOTAL										

1 Putt	2 Putts	3 Putts	Other	Total Putts	My Average # of Putts this Round

Eagles	Birdies	Pars	Bogeys	Double Bogeys	Snowmen (8s) or Other

DATE: Tee Time:

Green Fees: $ Walk or Ride?

Weather:

Course Par: Course Yardage:

USGA Course Rating: USGA Course Slope:

Members of Foursome:

Notes:

Hole	Par	Yards	Handicap	Fairways Hit in Regulation	Greens Hit in Regulation	# of Putts	My Score	Player #2 _____ Score	Player #3 _____ Score	Player #4 _____ Score
1										
2										
3										
4										
5										
6										
7										
8										
9										
OUT										
10										
11										
12										
13										
14										
15										
16										
17										
18										
IN										
OUT										
TOTAL										

1 Putt	2 Putts	3 Putts	Other	Total Putts	My Average # of Putts this Round

Eagles	Birdies	Pars	Bogeys	Double Bogeys	Snowmen (8s) or Other

DATE: Tee Time:

Green Fees: $ Walk or Ride?

Weather:

Course Par: Course Yardage:

USGA Course Rating: USGA Course Slope:

Members of Foursome:

Notes:

Hole	Par	Yards	Handicap	Fairways Hit in Regulation	Greens Hit in Regulation	# of Putts	My Score	Player #2 Score	Player #3 Score	Player #4 Score
1										
2										
3										
4										
5										
6										
7										
8										
9										
OUT										
10										
11										
12										
13										
14										
15										
16										
17										
18										
IN										
OUT										
TOTAL										

1 Putt	2 Putts	3 Putts	Other	Total Putts	My Average # of Putts this Round

Eagles	Birdies	Pars	Bogeys	Double Bogeys	Snowmen (8s) or Other

DATE: Tee Time:

Green Fees: $ Walk or Ride?

Weather:

Course Par: Course Yardage:

USGA Course Rating: USGA Course Slope:

Members of Foursome:

Notes:

Hole	Par	Yards	Handicap	Fairways Hit in Regulation	Greens Hit in Regulation	# of Putts	My Score	Player #2 Score	Player #3 Score	Player #4 Score
1										
2										
3										
4										
5										
6										
7										
8										
9										
OUT										
10										
11										
12										
13										
14										
15										
16										
17										
18										
IN										
OUT										
TOTAL										

1 Putt	2 Putts	3 Putts	Other	Total Putts	My Average # of Putts this Round

Eagles	Birdies	Pars	Bogeys	Double Bogeys	Snowmen (8s) or Other

DATE: Tee Time:

Green Fees: $ Walk or Ride?

Weather:

Course Par: Course Yardage:

USGA Course Rating: USGA Course Slope:

Members of Foursome:

Notes:

Hole	Par	Yards	Handicap	Fairways Hit in Regulation	Greens Hit in Regulation	# of Putts	My Score	Player #2 _____ Score	Player #3 _____ Score	Player #4 _____ Score
1										
2										
3										
4										
5										
6										
7										
8										
9										
OUT										
10										
11										
12										
13										
14										
15										
16										
17										
18										
IN										
OUT										
TOTAL										

1 Putt	2 Putts	3 Putts	Other	Total Putts	My Average # of Putts this Round

Eagles	Birdies	Pars	Bogeys	Double Bogeys	Snowmen (8s) or Other

GOLF LOG

DATE: Tee Time:

Green Fees: $ Walk or Ride?

Weather:

Course Par: Course Yardage:

USGA Course Rating: USGA Course Slope:

Members of Foursome:

Notes:

Hole	Par	Yards	Handicap	Fairways Hit in Regulation	Greens Hit in Regulation	# of Putts	My Score	Player #2 ___ Score	Player #3 ___ Score	Player #4 ___ Score
1										
2										
3										
4										
5										
6										
7										
8										
9										
OUT										
10										
11										
12										
13										
14										
15										
16										
17										
18										
IN										
OUT										
TOTAL										

1 Putt	2 Putts	3 Putts	Other	Total Putts	My Average # of Putts this Round

Eagles	Birdies	Pars	Bogeys	Double Bogeys	Snowmen (8s) or Other

DATE: _____   Tee Time: _____

Green Fees: $ _____   Walk or Ride? _____

Weather: _____

Course Par: _____   Course Yardage: _____

USGA Course Rating: _____   USGA Course Slope: _____

Members of Foursome: _____

Notes: _____

Hole	Par	Yards	Handicap	Fairways Hit in Regulation	Greens Hit in Regulation	# of Putts	My Score	Player #2 ___ Score	Player #3 ___ Score	Player #4 ___ Score
1										
2										
3										
4										
5										
6										
7										
8										
9										
OUT										
10										
11										
12										
13										
14										
15										
16										
17										
18										
IN										
OUT										
TOTAL										

1 Putt	2 Putts	3 Putts	Other	Total Putts	My Average # of Putts this Round

Eagles	Birdies	Pars	Bogeys	Double Bogeys	Snowmen (8s) or Other

MY FAVORITE ROUNDS OF GOLF

Keep your favorite scorecards and golf memories here.

GOLF COURSE:_____

DATE: Tee Time:

Green Fees: $ Walk or Ride?

Weather:

Course Par: Course Yardage:

USGA Course Rating: USGA Course Slope:

Members of Foursome:

Notes:

> *When I die, bury me
> on the golf course so
> my husband will visit.*
>
> —Author Unknown

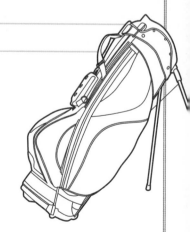

ATTACH SCORECARD HERE

GOLF COURSE:_____

DATE: Tee Time:

Green Fees: $ Walk or Ride?

Weather:

Course Par: Course Yardage:

USGA Course Rating: USGA Course Slope:

Members of Foursome:

Notes:

_____

_____

_____

_____

_____

_____

> *They call it golf*
> *because all of the*
> *other four-letter*
> *words were taken.*
>
> —Raymond Floyd

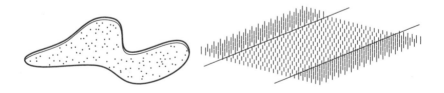

ATTACH SCORECARD HERE

GOLF COURSE:_____

DATE:_____ Tee Time:_____

Green Fees: $_____ Walk or Ride?_____

Weather:_____

Course Par:_____ Course Yardage:_____

USGA Course Rating:_____ USGA Course Slope:_____

Members of Foursome:_____

Notes:_____

_____

_____

_____

_____

_____

_____

_____

_____

> *Golf is a game that is played on a five-inch course—the distance between your ears.*
>
> —Bobby Jones Jr.

ATTACH SCORECARD HERE

MY HOLE-IN-ONE

Shooting a hole-in-one is one of the hardest feats in sports and, for most golfers, the ultimate dream. And here—skillful, talented, and lucky you—you have achieved it! Congratulations!

Golf Course:

Hole #:

Yardage:

Club Used:

Date:

Witnesses:

ATTACH SCORECARD OR PHOTO HERE

GOLF TOURNAMENTS

Whether you are a serious golfer or a weekend hacker, playing in tournaments is always entertaining and rewarding. Many golf tournaments are set up as networking events or to raise money for a charity. Check your local course for tournament listings, or go online and search for tournaments at other courses in your area.

Below, you can keep track of the tournaments you've played in and any awards you've won (longest drive, longest putt, putting contest, etc)

TOURNAMENTS I'VE PLAYED IN:

TOURNAMENT:

Golf Course:

Date:

Score:

Award:

TOURNAMENT:

Golf Course:

Date:

Score:

Award:

TOURNAMENT:

Golf Course:

Date:

Score:

Award:

> *It took me seventeen years to get 3,000 hits in baseball. I did it in one afternoon on the golf course.*
> —Hank Aaron

TOURNAMENT:

Golf Course:

Date:

Score:

Award:

TOURNAMENT:

Golf Course:

Date:

Score:

Award:

TOURNAMENT:

Golf Course:

Date:

Score:

Award:

PROFESSIONAL GOLF TOURNAMENTS I'VE ATTENDED

While watching golf on television is always engaging (although nongolfers may disagree), attending a professional tournament is amazing and inspirational. Watching professional golfers hit a golf ball in person is an incredible experience, whether they are teeing off or simply tapping a two-foot putt. By walking the course and following your favorite players, you gain insight into the real world of professional golf—the one that doesn't always transmit through your television. Concentration. Force. Focus. Perserverance. Luck.

> *I know I am getting better at golf because I'm hitting fewer spectators.*
>
> —Gerald Ford

TOURNAMENT:

Date: Cost:

Professionals I Followed During the Day:

ATTACH TOURNAMENT ENTRANCE TAGS HERE

TOURNAMENT:

Date: Cost:

Professionals I Followed During the Day:

ATTACH TOURNAMENT ENTRANCE TAGS HERE

TOURNAMENT:

Date: Cost:

Professionals I Followed During the Day:

ATTACH TOURNAMENT ENTRANCE TAGS HERE

MY FAVORITE 19TH HOLES

The 19th Hole is a post-round clubhouse happy hour or snack that is a tradition most golfers enjoy. Every golfer has a favorite 19th Hole, and the day usually is not complete until he or she ends up in the clubhouse for drinks and something to eat. It's a time to sit down with other golfers and compare the day—the great shots, the sad misses, and if you are a competitive group, it's a perfect opportunity to start arguing about who actually shot the lowest score.

LOCATION:

Address:

Hours:

Best Menu Items:

Best Cocktail or Beer:

LOCATION:

Address:

Hours:

Best Menu Items:

Best Cocktail or Beer:

> *If you drink, don't drive. Don't even putt.*
> —Dean Martin

LOCATION:

Address:

Hours:

Best Menu Items:

Best Cocktail or Beer:

LOCATION:

Address:

Hours:

Best Menu Items:

Best Cocktail or Beer:

LOCATION:

Address:

Hours:

Best Menu Items:

Best Cocktail or Beer:

LOCATION:

Address:

Hours:

Best Menu Items:

Best Cocktail or Beer:

LOCATION:

Address:

Hours:

Best Menu Items:

Best Cocktail or Beer:

Not only are you addicted to golf, but you are crazy for math. Right? Most golfers don't know how to compute their golf handicap, but don't let the math scare you. Recent data reveals that only 21 percent of golfers have a real handicap, with men averaging 15 and women averaging 28. In the United States, the average golf score is 95 for men and 106 for women.

TO ESTABLISH YOUR GOLF HANDICAP

STEP 1: Fill in a minimum of five scores and a maximum of 20.

Use the following chart to keep track of your latest rounds of golf—you'll need at least five to calculate your handicap, and you can enter up to 20. Fill in the name of the course, the USGA Course Rating, the USGA Slope Rating, and your score. The USGA Course Rating gives scratch golfers a way to determine the difficulty of the course. The USGA

> *The other day I broke 70. That's a lot of clubs.*
>
> —Henny Youngman

Slope Rating is a measurement for bogey golfers to determine the difficulty of the course. The minimum Slope Rating is 55 and the maximum is 155—the average difficulty for a rated golf course is 113. These ratings are established for each set of tees on a golf course and should be listed on your scorecard.

ROUND	COURSE	MY SCORE	USGA COURSE RATING	USGA SLOPE RATING	STEP 2/ DIFFERENTIALS
1					
2					
3					
4					
5					
6					
7					
8					
9					
10					
11					
12					
13					
14					
15					
16					
17					
18					
19					
20					

STEP 2: Calculate the handicap differential for each round entered using the following formula:

(SCORE – USGA COURSE RATING) x 113 / USGA SLOPE RATING.

113 is the Slope Rating of standard difficulty. Calculate the differential for each round entered.

STEP 3: Decide how many differentials are going to be used. Not every differential calculated in Step 2 will be used here. If only five rounds are entered in Step 1, only the lowest differential will be used. If 20 rounds are entered, only the 10 lowest differentials are used. Use the following chart to determine how many differentials to use based on the number of scores you entered.

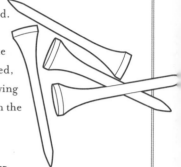

SCORES ENTERED IN STEP 1	DIFFERENTIALS USED
5–6	1 lowest
7–8	2 lowest
9–10	3 lowest
11–12	4 lowest
13–14	5 lowest
15–16	6 lowest
17	7 lowest
18	8 lowest
19	9 lowest
20	10 lowest

STEP 4: Calculate an average of the differentials used by adding them together and then dividing by the number used (i.e., if four differentials are used, add them up and divide by 4). Then multiply the result by 0.96 (96 percent). Drop all the digits after the tenths (do not round off); the result is your handicap index.

Example: Below are 7 scores played on the same golf course with the differentials calculated for each score:

SCORE	COURSE RATING	SLOPE RATING	DIFFERENTIAL
98	73.3	114	24.48
87	73.3	114	13.58
93	73.3	114	19.53
101	73.3	114	27.46
92	73.3	114	18.54
89	73.3	114	15.56
99	73.3	114	25.47

Next, take the two lowest differentials and average them:

$$13.58 + 15.56 / 2 = 21.36$$

Now multiply the result by 0.96, which equals 20.50653, and drop off the digits beyond the first decimal place. This is the handicap index.

$$21.36 \times .96 = 20.5$$

Honestly, it's far easier to do this with an online golf handicap calculator (available on numerous golf Web sites) or officially at your local golf course or country club. The USGA requires that you belong to a golf club (a group of ten members or more) in order to get an official golf handicap rating.

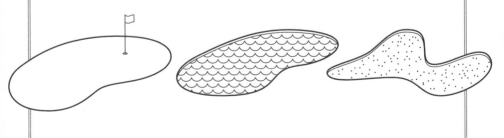

GOLF GAMES

STROKE PLAY OR MEDAL PLAY

This is standard play, in which every stroke during a round of golf counts and the lowest score wins.

MATCH PLAY

A round of play in which each hole is scored on a hole-by-hole basis. A hole is won by shooting the lowest score on that hole. The player or team winning the most holes wins the match.

GROSS GAME

All strokes count and there is no adjustment based on your handicap. The final score is the total number of strokes played.

NET GAME

This allows all players to compete on a level playing field. The net score is the gross score minus the player's handicap. In match play, the higher-handicap player will be allotted a number of strokes equal to the difference in handicaps between the lowest- and the highest-handicap players.

BEST BALL

The players divide into teams, with each golfer playing his or her own ball all the time. Only the lowest teammate's score is counted on each hole toward the team's round; the bad scores are ignored.

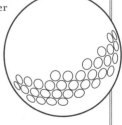

SCRAMBLE

In a foursome, every golfer hits from the tee. The best tee shot is then chosen, and the three other golfers pick up their ball. All four golfers then hit from the spot of the best tee shot. Only the shot selected as the best ball will count toward the stroke tally. This continues until the hole is finished. The entire round is played this way.

SHAMBLES

This is a combination of best ball and a scramble. Each player hits off the tee, and then the best tee shot is chosen. The three other golfers in the foursome must then drop their ball within one club length of the ball (but no nearer the hole). Each player then plays out the hole with his or her ball. Winner is the lowest score on the hole and the lowest score of the round. While in a foursome, you can also play this game as teams—two teams of two golfers. Each golfer hits a tee shot, and then each team selects the best tee shot of their individual team. Each player then finishes out the hole with his or her own ball, and the winner is the golfer with the lowest score on the hole and the round.

FEWEST PUTTS

This game is an easy one to follow—the winner is simply the player with the fewest number of putts in the round. Putts are counted only when the ball is on the green. If the ball is on the fringe and the golfer uses a putter, it does not count. If any part of the golf ball is on the green, it is considered fair and in play for this game.

ACEY-DUCEY

> *Golf is a game in which*
> *you yell "fore," shoot six,*
> *and write down five.*
>
> —Paul Harvey

This game is a lot of fun and always causes a lot of discord between players, as there is one clear winner, two modest losers, and one big-time loser for each hole. In a foursome, the low scorer on each hole wins a set amount from the three other players. The high scorer on each hole then has to pay the same to all three other players. This can really add up during the round, so there is a chance for one member of the foursome to be very upset and broke by the end.

BINGO BANGO BONGO

This is a great game that allows players with wide handicap differences to play a more competitive game. Players earn points based on the following criteria:

BINGO: First ball on the green = 1 point

BANGO: Closest ball to the pin = 1 point

BONGO: First ball to hole out = 1 point

Since one of the points can be earned by holing out, it's important that your group maintain the proper golf etiquette and allow the player farthest from the hole to always play first. You can also add a twist to this game by doubling the points when the same player wins all three points on a hole.

LONGEST YARD

The player who shoots the lowest score on the hole wins the equivalent point value of the yardage of the hole. For example, if you are playing a 485-yard hole, winning the hole would win you 485 points. The player with the most points at the end of the round wins.

NASSAU

> *Golf is like a love affair. If you don't take it seriously, it's no fun; if you do take it seriously, it breaks your heart.*
>
> —Arthur Daley

This is one of the most popular golf games because it is actually three games in one—the front nine, back nine, and overall 18-hole score all count as separate bets. In a Nassau Tournament, the player (or team) winning the front nine wins a bet or prize; the player (or team) winning the back nine wins a bet or prize; and the player or team with the low 18-hole score wins a bet or prize. A player or team sweeping all three wins it all—and you can have an additional bet for this occurrence. You can play stroke play or match play, and combine it with other games simultaneously.

PICK-UP STICKS

A challenging game that should only be played by two golfers with similar handicaps. Play match play, and the winner of each hole then takes one of his or her opponent's golf clubs. This club is then out of play for that player for the rest of the round. If you tie the hole, no clubs are taken away. At the start, each player may only carry the maximum of 14 clubs. This will make for many creative golf shots. You can decide before play begins whether or not your putter is "off limits."

ROUND ROBIN

This game is best played by golfers who are at a similar skill level since four players are needed. Round Robin pits each golfer against the other three—but at each hole you are teamed with one other golfer, so each hole is played two on two. Golfers rotate partners after every six holes so that each golfer plays with every other member of the foursome over the course of 18 holes. Match play or stroke play can be used, and after each six-hole segment, there can be a separate wager. If at the end of the 18 holes you've been on two winning sides and one losing side, you will come out ahead.

SKINS

An extremely popular game played for points or money, Skins pits players against each other in a type of match play where each hole has a set value ($1 per hole, for example). The player who wins the hole is said to "win the skin," which means he or she wins the set amount of points or dollars for the hole. Skins is often more dramatic than the usual match play because the holes are not halved. When players tie on a hole, the value of that hole is carried forward to the next hole—so if on the first hole you tied, the next hole would be worth 2 points or $2. The more ties, the greater the value of the skin and the bigger the eventual payoff.

OTHER BETS THAT MUST BE DETERMINED
BEFORE THE ROUND OF GOLF BEGINS

BARKIES: Set point value or dollar amount for any player hitting a tree during a hole and making par.

CHIPPIES: Set point value or dollar amount for any player chipping in from off the green—for a par or better.

SANDIES: Set point value or dollar amount for any player hitting out of a sand trap and making par.

ARNIES: *(named after Arnold Palmer)* Set point value or dollar amount for any player making par while not playing his ball in the fairway of the hole.

ABOUT THE AUTHOR

Lisa Bach hit her first golf ball when she was nine years old, and soon after was named *Golf Digest* Junior Player of the Year in Maryland. She has worked in book publishing for over fifteen years and is the editor of *Her Fork in the Road* and *365 Travel*. She has spent almost thirty years trying to hit a hole-in-one, and sadly, she's still trying.

ACKNOWLEDGMENTS

I love the game of golf, so I'm thrilled that my partner, Karen Verpeet, has decided to embrace the game as well. Karen has a gorgeous swing, and I fear that one day she will beat me. And when she does, it'll be my pleasure to buy her, and everyone at the 19th Hole, a drink. Karen—thanks for the happiness and the laughter, and for always saying (whether deserved or not), "nice shot."

My father, William Bach, used to wake me at the crack of dawn to go to our local golf course to play. We were always the first ones out on the course, and I loved sharing that time with him. My mother, Barbara Bach, always encouraged me, and to this day she still contends that I should have gone pro—but I guess that's what a mother is for. I am indebted to them both, as I know my first set of clubs set them back quite a bit—and thankfully, I'm still using them over 20 years later. I also appreciate the love and support of my family: Amy, Steve, Joshua, Jacob, Daniel and Jessica Volin and David, Laura, Aaron, and Noah Bach. I also want to acknowledge my incredible extended family, Hugo Verpeet, Evelien Verpeet, Matthew Certa, Anjes De Ryck, and Tom Simpson.

Gratitude and affection go out to my amazing friends: Kim Arnone, Jo Beaton, Kevin Bentley, Andie Bourget, Jeff Campbell, Leslie Davisson, Leisha Fry, Rachel Geiger, Phil Hahn, Laura Harger, Sandi Hassett, Robin Helbling, Daniel Jason, Sally Kim, Karen Levine, Deneil LoGiudice, Rachel Longan, Jennifer Nannini, Neil Perry, Deanna Quinones, Inge Schilperoord, Erica Smith, Jeremy Sterling, Mark Swiney, Tacy Trowbridge, and Beth Weber. I hope that all of you learn to play golf by the time we retire, so we'll be able to pull together a foursome on short notice—any day of the week.

Thanks to all the talented folks at Chronicle Books, especially Liz Rockhold, Jason Sacher, Megan Strahm, Eric Tallman, and Sarah Williams.

And finally, thanks to my editor, Mikyla Bruder, an old friend and colleague whom I have enormous respect for and who I hope will one day pick up a golf club and give the game a try.